THE BUSINESS
TRAVELLER'S TALES

THE BUSINESS TRAVELLER'S TALES

W. C. NG

w c ng

Contents

In memory of Ah Ma,
Who was much loved by us all.

About the Author

W C Ng is a finance professional with over 25 years of working experience in a multinational company. Embodied with a passion for writing and in connecting with people, coupled with an elephant's memory of long past events, "The Business Traveller's Tales" is a collection of stories from over two decades of business travel.

Preface and
Acknowledgements

Having been on business travels for over 2 decades, I have accumulated several stories and experiences that I have captured on notes scribbled over the years. The non-travelling years of 2020 and 2021 prompted me to reflect on these travels and the stories collected. I have also stepped off the career ladder at the end of 2020 (at least temporarily), and these developments have caused me to feel that this may be an opportune time to put these stories and thoughts into a book to share with fellow business travellers and with all who have missed the magic in business travelling, which has stopped for most when Covid-19 struck globally in 2020.

Business travel has always been considered a work perk in one's career. Be it millennials or older adults, everyone (or many, at least) loves the thrills in business travelling– travelling on company's expenses, taking flights on different airlines to visit new places, meeting people from different parts of the world, experiencing different hotels and restaurants, visiting tourist spots if time allows–it is a breakaway from the usually mundane life and work we go through daily. Business travel is also often seen as a status symbol–you have arrived on the world stage, or so it is assumed.

Whilst much of the world takes a pause on business travelling for now, I am certain business travelling will resume post Covid-19, but significant changes can be expected, and it would be interesting to see how business travel will evolve in the next few years. My belief is that business travel will not return to 2019 levels, as this "ongoing experiment" has shown that with advances in virtual technology, and considerations of cost and carbon emissions, business travel may be curtailed in the future. Let's see how this unfolds!

Prior to 2020, business travellers make up about 12% of the airplane's passengers, but they pull in as much as 75% of profits[1]. Global travel statistics from 2017 showed that $1.33 trillion was spent on business travel worldwide. In the United States, US travellers took over 463 million business trips inside the US in 2018[2].

Covid-19 put a stop to many forms of business travelling, and face-to-face meetings and chats are quickly replaced with video conferencing services such as Zoom, Teams, etc. It is fascinating to see how humans can quickly adapt to the changes and challenges posed. A new way of working from home came about, and office workers began to get used to reporting for work whilst sitting at the dining or study table, having social group conversations via online apps, arranging for virtual work lunches via video conferencing, etc. Many businesses may have folded due to the economic impact from Covid-19, but I doubt any did because its staff could not travel for business. This is one thing that the pandemic has taught us –you do not need to be at the office (not all the time at least) or to be constantly on the road to get work or business deals done.

I have a few to thank for enabling this book to be completed. To Lay Hong and Pak Kheng, thank you for the continued reminders over the years that you are waiting to read my first book. It felt good to know that you are supporting me in my author's dream, and for believing that I will someday do it!

I also thank my niece, Jaime, for the lovely illustrations she has incorporated into the chapters, my cousin-in-law Yumi for helping to edit the initial version of the book, and my cousin Daryl for assisting to get it published. It is truly a family effort, and I am sure our late Ah Ma would be very proud and happy that we have remained a closely knit family even after she has left us.

I thank my parents and my husband for their unconditional love and support. I know I will always be your precious, no matter if I am five or fifty years old!

Lastly, I thank my ex-company. I joined the company as an insecure young adult and left as a confident middle-aged woman. The last 25 years have been a blast, with the opportunities, exposures, and challenges that have been presented through the course of work, and I would not have been able to write this book without the business trips that I have taken in the company's name. I did a count–I have visited at least 23 countries (and many cities) on business travel in the past two decades.

Life is all about the unique experiences we have encountered. Be it for leisure or business, travelling allows us to get new experiences, gain new insights, and meet people, even though we may cross paths with most only briefly and never see them again.

I share my business travelling tales with you and I hope reading them will trigger your own memories of your business travelling experiences!

I am very grateful to all who have bought the book. Thank you all.

Chapter 1

Candies Convey Love and a Goody Bag of Snacks Can Mean Survival

" A Piece Of Candy Never Fails To Warm The Heart & Soothe The Lonely Soul."

Does getting a box of candies trigger a spark of joy in your eyes and warm the cockles of your heart? For me, it does, immediately! Getting a piece of candy from a friend or a loved one is like receiving their blessing of love. The taste of some candies may even remind you of childhood days of long ago, of sitting with friends at the playground, chatting and enjoying different candies whilst watching the world go by. Ouch, the sweet innocence of childhood, now lost.

One morning, when I was six years old and was preparing to go to school, my grandmother (we addressed her as "Ah Ma") gave me a honey lemon Hudson's sweet to take to school. I had just started primary school life a few days before and was still having the jitters. I could speak Teochew (a Chinese dialect) and some Mandarin but knew little English. (This inability to converse fluently in English, and my struggle with the correct pronunciation, racked my self-confidence for years. I still recall the hurt I felt when my classmates laughed at me for pronouncing 'library' as 'libralie', but that was how my mother pronounced it and I had followed suit.) "Have it when you are feeling nervous", Ah Ma said. Over four decades later, I still remember that moment—I love you, Ah Ma!

The morning classes went well, and then it was recess. I was all right after all and had even made some small talk with my new classmates! The late morning classes continued. Midway through my Chinese language class, I suddenly remembered that the Hudson's sweet was still in my pocket. "Oh dear, Ah Ma will be disappointed if I do not eat her candy", my six-year-old mind thought innocently and suddenly became disturbed. I did not want Ah Ma to think that I did not appreciate her gift. Without a second thought, I took the sweet out of my pocket and popped it into my mouth.

Wrong move. My teacher spotted it immediately, and I was told to spit it out and throw it into the garbage bin, with the entire class looking at me. "You should know you are not allowed to eat during class!" Tsk tsk. Not the impression a new student should give her teacher, but hey, she did not know the caring story behind the Hudson's honey lemon sweet.

Fast forward a few decades and one thing has remained unchanged. Even though I do not have a sweet tooth and seldom eat sweets, I still associate a box of candies with love and care, and all Hudson's sweets remind me of my grandmother's love!

All children love sweets, and well, so do many adults. Chocolate, for example, is often associated with romance, and it is no surprise that it is a common gift on Valentine's Day—it is hard for anyone to say no to chocolates! Chocolate contains several compounds linked to mood-lifting chemicals in the brain[3]. However, a study has proposed that it is more the experience of eating chocolate, and satisfying a food craving, that releases endorphins and the feel-good chemical dopamine [4]. Another study also proposes that feelings of love can actually come from sweets[5]! Bottom line is, eating chocolates and other sweets makes you feel happy and loved, and they can conjure up romantic feelings in some hearts!

When my husband S and I first got together, he used to travel regularly for business. S has no qualms about flying but sometimes feels queasy as he prepares to go to the airport and when he gets onto the airplane. He is fine once the airplane takes off though.

As a fellow business traveller, I understand how it feels like to travel alone, and the way anxiety can sometimes get a hold of us. As S likes candy, I would always pack him a candy goody bag to take with him. In the paper bag, he would find his favourite sweets and mints, the brand of chocolates that he likes, and some packets of biscuits. I would also slip in a note of encouragement, and sometimes, an empty red packet for good luck.

He does the same for me when I travel—and mine is a different type of goody bag! I am less keen on sweets, but I do like potato chips and preserved or candied fruits, especially ginger, as I am prone to motion sickness and ginger has been proven to be effective against nausea[6]. I also like dark chocolates and nuts. For biscuits, he gets me my favourite Teochew pastry, sweet and salty *tau sar pia* (a Chinese type of pastry with a sweet or savoury bean paste filling)—yummy!

Opening my goody bag during the flight and taking bites during the trip never fails to put a smile on my face and a warm fuzzy feeling in my heart. It is a caring gesture that makes me feel very much loved and cherished. You do not feel so lonely and homesick anymore. It almost feels as though the giver is there with you as you visit different parts of the world. Also, no matter how far away you may be from home, home does not seem that far away when you have your favourite hometown treats and snacks with you!

On a separate note, but still on the theme of candies, I should mention that my mother gave me an important piece of advice regarding candies when I first started out in my career. "On your first day at a new job or company, bring a bag of sweets to share with your new colleagues. This will ensure that they will only have sweet and good things to say about you going forward." I am not sure how true this is, and I have not followed it faithfully, but well, no harm in trying—it may well help you in your career, and if not, at least everyone got to try some sweets!

Candies mean love, and love is sweet. Just like the candy my grandmother gave me when I was six.

SHARING TIP!

Give a goody bag to a loved one or friend who is travelling on business – they will love you for it!

May be a good idea to bring a box of candies to share with new colleagues on your first day at work. You never know, it may help you to have harmonious relationships in the workplace.

Chapter 2

Staying Healthy
While on The Road

"Eating Well Is Important But Eating Safely Is Paramount."

Any seasoned business traveller will tell you that the two most important goals while on the road are: 1) stay healthy, and 2) avoid falling sick.

Some people have bodies that are built for travelling and can withstand any tough conditions—they adjust easily to any time zone and take to the local conditions and food quickly. Then, there are others whose bodies are only built for home ground conditions and are not as adaptable to changes. Well, that describes my body. I have a sensitive stomach. I do not sleep well when I travel (more about this in the next chapter). I am susceptible to motion sickness, and I worry about catching germs. Hardly the archetype of a seasoned business traveller!

Keeping the germs away

I am quite like Naomi Campbell[7] when it comes to sanitization. Upon getting to my seat on the airplane, I will use a wet tissue or the hot towel given by the flight attendant to wipe my seat first, then the remote control, the tray, and finally the handles. Upon entering my hotel room, the second thing I do (after checking out the evacuation route, see Chapter 4) is to take out my wet wipes and clean the toilet bowl, tap, remote control, and room telephone. Call me a scaredy-cat, but these 5-minute routines give me some peace of mind.

Exercising

With most business trips being mainly about going to the airport, hotel, and office, followed by the evening dinner, which never ends by 9 pm, one has little personal time for oneself, much less to exercise or be physically active.

Some colleagues are regular gym bunnies, and they will show up at the hotel gym first thing in the morning, regardless of when they hit the sack the night before. I do not go to the gym (I do not fancy waking up early for a workout or having people watching me doing a workout). Interestingly, some colleagues told me they only go to the gym when they travel ("No time to do so back home. The kids take up all my time.") I also learned that if you want to get into the good books of the gym-going senior business head, or if there is an issue you want to discuss with him or her but could not squeeze in an appointment, one way is to show up at the gym at 5 am and you may get lucky. Well, should

you climb up the career ladder after picking up this tip, remember you first read it here!

I started exercising regularly when I stepped into my 40s, and when I travel, I try to keep to my short daily exercise routine. I usually start with some yoga breathing exercises and stretching, followed by ten minutes of HIIT (high-intensity interval training)—star jumps, running on the spot, planks, squats, burpees, skipping, etc. This takes up only a few minutes of the morning, pumps up the heart, and fires up the muscles—a great way to start the day. Try it!

The other important point to note is that work is not your life. Being overseas on a corporate account does not mean you are obligated to eat, drink, walk and sleep thinking of work all the time. Your eyes and mind will need a break; you are not a corporate slave. Allocating personal time to connect with family or simply for relaxation is a crucial component to keeping a healthy state of mind, which is as important as your physical health.

Getting over motion sickness

I have been prone to motion sickness since I was young. Motion sickness causes a feeling of sickness that is triggered by movement, which happens when there is conflict among the senses[8]. Once triggered, motion sickness activates, in my case, dizziness and nausea. I am almost certain to get it when I am on a boat, and sometimes during car rides, but luckily less so when I am on a plane. During long car rides, some colleagues would take out their phones or laptops and start working away, but I am unable to do so, as doing this would surely make me carsick. All I can do is sit back, look out of the window, and enjoy the scenery, which is not a bad thing really, as this may be the only opportunity to take in the local sights.

That said, over the years I have found some aids that work for me! I wear travel sickness bands (acupressure bands that fit around your wrist) when I am on the road, and my medicine kit always contains some motion sickness pills. One problem solved, thankfully.

Eating right

The next thing to watch is to eat right and healthy, which can be hard when you are on the road and with all meals on the company's account. It is hard to control greed for food—business travel can turn one into a glutton, which leads to a higher risk of obesity! Then there are travellers who would only go to expensive restaurants, or order the most expensive dishes on the menu, and have excellent wine. I often wondered if they did so only because they did not have to pay for the dinner from their own pocket. I must admit I used to view such travellers with a bit of disdain. My husband, however, offered an alternative view on this, which I think makes some sense. Business travel takes people away from their family and personal commitments—the good meals are compensation for the personal sacrifice they have to make. That is one way of looking at it. Another way is to see it as a privilege, I suppose.

I am not a foodie and, in fact, I can be a picky eater, much to the annoyance of my dining companions. I try out the local delicacies on the menu if I think I am game for it, or if the restaurant is known for a certain dish, but otherwise, my food choices are usually standard boring fare.

That said, I had a gluttony issue when I started travelling for work. My "Achilles' heel" is the morning breakfast, which is the highlight of my day. The thought of a warm, sumptuous breakfast—toasted bread with jam, fried eggs, bacon, hash brown, roasted potatoes, sausages, sometimes a waffle, and a nice big cup of coffee (Gosh, writing this has given me a sudden craving for a hotel breakfast!)—never fails to motivate me to get out of bed, even if I have had little or bad sleep the night before. I am usually not a big breakfast eater, and at home, my breakfast is very light, but for some strange reason, I am a different person when I travel (yes, it is greed).

As the volume of business travel increased, or as I got older (or perhaps a combination of both), it hit me one morning at breakfast that I could not afford to continue eating my substantial "hotel breakfast" portions and yet be able to maintain my weight and health—something had to give, and it would not be my health.

Since then, whenever I travel, I have a "standard" menu which I stick to dutifully. If it is a hotel in Asia (or one that serves mainly Chinese food), I would go for a bowl of porridge, fried eggs, tofu, some bacon strips, and some vegetables. If it is a Western-style hotel, it would be a bowl of plain cereal with a banana and some nuts thrown in, plus a side plate of fried eggs. Sticking to a fixed menu mindset removes decision making—you know exactly what to go for and steel yourself away from the temptation of pancakes, sausages, cakes, etc. It also enables a quick selection process, which is important, for as we know, the time we have for breakfast is usually short. Having said that, I still uphold my "hotel breakfast" portions when I travel on holiday—I am on holiday after all!

Food Safety

Eating at different hotels has resulted in some interesting stories, especially relating to food hygiene. Food safety is something I pay attention to, given my weak stomach, and it is dreadful to be sick from food poisoning, especially when you are on the road.

There was one breakfast at my usual London hotel that I remembered well. I had asked the waitress for a boiled egg (the hotel was undergoing some renovations, and guests had to send in orders rather than help themselves at the buffet table). The egg came, and I peeled it open, only to be horrified by what was inside. I took a double look to make sure I had seen what I thought I saw—small feathers and what looked like an unborn chick inside the egg! Petrified and starting to feel sick to the stomach, I did not check further.

Well, I know such eggs can be a delicacy in countries like the Philippines and Cambodia. (Known as *balut*, it is a hard-boiled egg with a partially formed duck foetus inside[9].) I had seen stalls selling it in these countries, but there was no way I could bring myself near them, much less eat balut! The thought of a poor chick almost making it to life but not making it in the end, is a terrifying one (though it is strange I do not find it frightening that a chick that makes it to life often ends up on the dinner table). That said, balut is considered a highly nutritious dish and can be a mini meal that creates a lot of heat and energy in the body.

I showed the egg to the waitress who served me, and she too took a second look, bewildered and speechless. She took it back to the kitchen straight away and came back with a new boiled egg but could not explain the reason for the abnormal egg. By then, I had suddenly developed a phobia of eggs that stayed with me for a few months. If you Google "chicken foetus in my egg" you will find images and stories similar to mine—I suppose it is a very rare occurrence, but it does happen!

Then, there was my first business trip to Chennai, India, in 2008, which I went along with a colleague. Not knowing what to expect and having heard stories about food poisoning, we went fully geared. We stocked up on snacks and biscuits and many bottles of mineral water, which filled up most of our luggage.

Throughout the trip, we scrutinised everything we ate carefully. No salad, no ice cubes, and we only ordered cooked food that was prepared with fresh ingredients. Bottled water was available everywhere we went, but we only drank Pepsi bottled mineral water, as we had heard (unverified) stories of unscrupulous vendors filling up used bottles with tap water and selling them as newly bottled mineral water. My colleague took the safety hygiene measures one notch higher—she even brushed her teeth and washed her hair using mineral water so that her mouth and eyes would not touch any tap water at all. Well, thankfully, nothing happened on that trip or the next few trips. We did, however, hear of a colleague who came down with food poisoning, and he suspected he got that from inadvertently drinking a few mouthfuls of water from the hotel pool whilst swimming.

Unfortunately, I had an episode of food poisoning—in 2019, during one of my trips to China, and it was a rather severe case of diarrhoea and vomiting.

I had my usual breakfast of rice porridge with fried eggs and some preserved vegetables, though that morning I added a few spoonfuls of fried silverfish (I suspect it was this that made me sick). Everything tasted normal and fine. The first inkling that something was not right started at about 10 am, shortly after the meeting started. I began to feel unwell and nauseous, and I initially thought it might be a case of indigestion. By 10:30 am, I felt that I was about to throw up and excused myself to go to my room.

I became violently ill soon after, with vomiting and diarrhoea. My colleagues were concerned and quickly arranged for me to go to the local hospital (China does not have general practitioner clinics as we do in Singapore). Two local female colleagues accompanied me. I was embarrassed to inconvenience them and for taking them away from their work, but they were very kind and told me not to worry. At the hospital, one colleague took my passport and joined the queue to register me, whilst the other stayed with me. We even made a joke—the lady who helped to register me said the receptionist remembered her and asked why she kept bringing foreigners to the hospital (a fellow director had visited the same hospital on a previous trip, suffering from a bad back.) We had a good laugh.

It was a brief wait and consultation. The bill came up to 50 RMB (S$10)—way too cheap, I thought! We made our way back to the hotel, and I rested for the rest of the day. The diarrhoea started to ease off, but the vomiting continued. I was feeling very sorry for myself and wishing that I was home rather than being alone in a hotel room.

By then, the hotel staff had heard about my illness and called to apologise. They also sent a bowl of porridge (no side dishes this time) when they heard that I had eaten nothing the whole day. My colleagues encouraged me to at least

drink the porridge water even if I could not swallow the rice. I tried to have some, but the nausea continued.

I had to miss the committee meeting the next day, but felt that I was well enough to join the team for the return trip home after the meeting. I also did not want to be left behind or to have to trouble a colleague to stay behind to look after me. By then the diarrhoea had stopped, though I still had bouts of vomiting.

The homeward journey was not a simple case of heading to the airport to catch a flight. We had to take a 3-hour road trip, making our way to Shenzhen, walking across the border to Hong Kong and continuing the car journey to Hong Kong International Airport. The journey that day has got to be one of the most unpleasant journeys I have ever had. I vomited in the car, and on the flight, I dared not eat anything and kept my eyes closed the entire time, willing myself not to be nauseous.

I have never felt as relieved as I did when I reached home that evening. I saw my GP the following day, and it took me another few days to recover, causing me to cancel a planned holiday, which was, ironically, to another part of China.

When I finally felt better and had the time to take a good look at the medicine given to me in China, I googled the English translation for the name of the pills in the medicine bag. That was when I discovered the doctor had not given me any medicine to stop the vomiting! Well, that explained the continued vomiting. I lost over 2 kgs that week, and my full appetite only came back days after.

Because of that episode, I have since stopped eating the porridge side dishes from that hotel, or any other hotel. Stick to the food that you know would be required to be freshly cooked. Even if porridge with side dishes is your favourite comfort food. This is how a traumatic experience changes you!

SHARING TIP!

Ensure you give yourself ample personal time during business trips. Your mind needs a rest from work!

Do act on your physical health and make it a routine to do some daily exercises. Even if it's only for 5 minutes. Five minutes is better than zero minutes.

Chapter 3

Why Is It So Difficult to Fall Asleep?

"Getting A Good Night's Sleep Can Sometimes Be A Pipe Dream."

Eating well and staying healthy is key when travelling, and I would add that sleeping well is just as important! When I started travelling for work, I was probably one of the lousiest travellers out there.

I slept poorly on short regional trips even though there was no time zone difference between Singapore and the country I was visiting. I suspected it was because I had difficulty adjusting to sleeping in a strange bed or being alone in a big room. Thankfully, this issue disappeared after some time, but new ones emerged when I started travelling further afar.

Two things worry me whenever I make intercontinental trips. One, that I will be unable to sleep during a night flight; and two, that I will experience jet lag at my destination or upon my return to Singapore.

On night flights, despite having the comfort of a lie-flat business class seat, I always struggled to get some quality sleep. I marvelled at those who can fall asleep and start snoring within minutes of the plane taking off—oh boy, am I envious that they can drift off to dreamland so easily! There must be a trick or skill to this, one which, despite almost 20 years of travel, I have yet to master.

That said, I have improved over the years, and whilst I still cannot sleep for the bulk of the flight, I am now usually able to catch about five to six hours of sleep out of a fourteen-hour flight. Here are my 'going to sleep' hacks on a night flight:

- Adjust your watch to your destination country's time zone once you board the plane. This helps to adjust your mind to get used to thinking about time in the new time zone.
- Change into loose and comfortable sleepwear after take-off. For me, this is usually some long-sleeved lounge wear and comfortable pants. Some airlines provide lounge wear that is comfortable and fashionable.
- Skip dinner or supper—if you say yes to having a meal, it will be at least three hours later before you can get to sleep. It is also difficult to sleep with a full tummy. Yes, do not be greedy!
- Use earplugs and eye masks. They really help me in blocking out noise and light and are my must-haves for any trip.
- For a luxurious feel, sometimes I spray some lavender essential oil on the pillow. Apart from the delightful smell, lavender is also known for its relaxing effects.
- If you feel cold on the plane, ask for an extra blanket. Keeping warm helps one in settling down to sleep.
- Do some deep breathing and relaxation exercises before you go to bed.

My issue with jet lag has proven difficult to shake off despite two decades of travel. Flying westward to Europe or eastward to North America rarely poses much of a sleep pattern issue. I typically fly out to Europe in the morning of Singapore time and arrive at my destination in the late afternoon. I stay active, do not take a nap, and after a light early dinner, I can usually knock off by ten in the evening. For the rest of the trip, I may wake up once or twice in the night, but I have no complaints, as, by and large, I can get enough sleep and rest during these trips.

It is returning to Singapore from an intercontinental flight that can sometimes trigger a bout of insomnia for me. Jet lag is a temporary disorder that causes fatigue, insomnia, and other symptoms as a result of air travel across multiple time zones.

Some say that it takes a day to recover for each hour of the time difference[10].

My worst experience with jet lag happened after returning home from a trip to the United States. I could not sleep, or slept very little, for over three weeks. It was a living nightmare, lying in bed every night tossing and turning, not sleeping a wink. With each passing sleepless night, the stress level increased, which made going to bed the next evening an even more worrying affair.

Sleep deprivation can turn you into an irritable monster. During the day, my head felt as heavy as if a brick were hanging on top of it. My work and life suffered. I tried everything—taking melatonin, doing exercises, drinking warm honey and chamomile tea before bedtime, counting sheep at night, meditation. Nothing worked. On that occasion, I had no choice but to see a doctor for some sleeping medication.

I continued to suffer from varying degrees of jet lag after some of my intercontinental flights, but it seemed to have improved with time, or, perhaps, age? I have also discovered a non-prescription drug available at pharmacies in the UK that contains diphenhydramine hydrochloride. I take it on nights when I have remained awake past midnight. It does not work all the time, but even achieving a 50% effective rate is good enough for me.

An important thing I have discovered is that the timing of my return flight matters. Ideally, if I am flying back from Europe, I should take an evening flight so that I can arrive in Singapore just before dusk. This arrival timing seems to cause the least jet lag effects for me as compared to other flight timings. I wished I had realized this earlier!

I read an article recently that shared tips from the US military on how to fall asleep in two minutes[11]. The technique is said to work for 96 percent of people after six weeks of practice:

1. Relax the muscles in your face, including the tongue, jaw, and the muscles around the eyes.
2. Drop your shoulders as far down as they will go, followed by your upper and lower arm, one side at a time.
3. Breathe out, relaxing your chest then your legs, starting from the thighs and going down.
4. You should then spend 10 seconds trying to clear your mind before thinking about one of the three following images:

   - You are lying in a canoe on a calm lake with nothing but a clear blue sky above you.
   - You are lying in a black velvet hammock in a pitch-black room.
   - You say "don't think, don't think, don't think" to yourself over and over for about 10 seconds.

Good night (fingers crossed), sleep well, and pleasant dreams!

SHARING TIP!

Try the US military tips on falling asleep in 2 minutes.

The timing of your flight can influence your sleep pattern.

Chapter 4

What Do You Do When the Siren Goes Off?

"Choosing Safety Is A Choice Of Life Over Career – Warren Farrell"

I did not have a good start to my two-week stay in London in 2008 at a new hotel that had commenced operations just barely a week before. (Note of advice: wait at least six months for a new hotel to sort out any teething issues before you make a booking!)

First, there were some computer system issues at check-in, and I had to wait quite a while before getting my room key. Once in my room, and after unpacking everything from my bags, the power suddenly went off, and the room went pitch dark. I called the concierge for help, and the staff came promptly to investigate, but after 30 minutes or so, the staff gave up trying to fix the issue and offered to put me in another room. An attendant then helped me to move my (let me highlight - **already unpacked**) stuff to another room on another floor. I was feeling pretty upset and worn out by then.

Well, the saga continued. Around eleven in the evening, when I was already in dreamland, the fire alarm went off and woke me up abruptly. By now I was really fed up with the hotel, and given the number of technical issues I had experienced so far, I brushed this off as another teething technical issue for the new hotel and went back to sleep.

However, the alarm continued to ring incessantly, so it was impossible to get back to sleep. After a while, I started to feel worried and wondered if it was indeed a genuine alarm. I opened the door, but neither saw nor smelt anything unusual in the corridor. I called the reception desk. Someone finally picked it up after several rings. I asked if the fire alarm had been triggered by a real incident. "Yes! What are you doing, why are you still in your room? Come down right now!"

By now, I was definitely in panic mode. I looked around the room—what should I take with me? I had never had to evacuate from a hotel before (the only time I had experienced an evacuation was when my family and I had to leave our flat in Singapore one night because of a huge tremor caused by an earthquake in Indonesia. What was memorable about that experience was that after we had assembled in the street along with dozens of other households, we realized that the whole family including our two dogs were there, but we had forgotten to wake my younger brother, so he was still asleep in bed. We had a good laugh afterwards, and no, we did not return to get him as we realised that there was no real danger.) With no time to think, I grabbed my handbag, which had my passport, put on a blazer, and rushed down the stairs. Upon exiting the hotel's doors, the brutal winter wind cut through the blazer to my bones, and I immediately shivered uncontrollably. I had forgotten it was winter! Scores of people were standing outside, and I asked one guy if he knew what the issue was. It was a small kitchen fire, he shared.

Gosh, I could have killed myself with my stupidity for not obeying the golden rule to evacuate as soon as the siren sounded off. And I doubled up my stupidity by rushing out with no socks on a winter evening and wearing only pyjamas and a light blazer. It was a freaking frosty night, and I tried to work up some heat by pacing up and down the side street.

Thankfully, we were allowed to go back to our rooms not long after. The rest of the stay was smooth with no other incidents, and I learned a valuable lesson about what to do if a hotel siren or fire alarm ever goes off. Since then, I always go to bed with my handbag (which has my passport and wallet) and phone next to my bed, within easy reach even in the dark.

I was on vacation in Italy with my husband a few years ago and, again, I experienced a fire alarm going off at our hotel on an early morning at about 8 am. This time, I reacted quickly. I grabbed my bag, wore the right clothing, and we got out of the room in less than two minutes. When I opened our room door, I was momentarily confused as I saw a second set of doors. Then I realized that the fire doors that lined the corridor outside our room had automatically closed, as they should whenever a fire alarm goes off. Thank God it was in the morning and there was light. I imagined I would be confused if this had happened in total darkness. I opened that door and we headed immediately for the stairs. (See the Appendix for more safety tips—checking out the fire exits upon check-in.)

The alarm had gone off at breakfast time, and a few guests carried their bread and coffee to the outside grounds—smart move! Scanning the crowd, I noticed a wide range of clothing being worn by the hotel guests. Most were appropriately dressed for the weather, in jeans and coats or jackets, though there was this brave chap who came in his bathroom robe (this was in October). I give him full credits for taking the siren seriously. A few had their carry-on luggage with them. They were either checking out when the siren sounded or had mastered the art of packing in 5 minutes! Twenty minutes or so later, I saw a family walking out of the door carrying their luggage and fully dressed in coats, hats, and scarves. I told my husband that if this had been an actual fire, they may not have been able to make it out in that fashion—I wondered what had been in their minds when they heard the siren!

Thankfully, other than these two incidents, I have not encountered any other safety-related incidents in a hotel. Some countries I have been to may not be considered the safest of places, but never once have I felt unsafe or that my safety was threatened.

By courtesy of travelling with a director of a board, I experienced a VIP safety service treatment once on a trip to a particular country. The director was accorded full safety protocol, with bodyguards accompanying us the minute we arrived at the airport until the point we left for the airport. Having the bodyguards wherever we went somehow made me feel more guarded and uncomfortable, and subconsciously thinking if there indeed was danger, which obviously was not the case. Well, I was free to roam on my next trip when the director did not travel with me. (I know, it implied that his life was much more valuable than mine!)

Then there were my travels to another country, whereby the Travel Advisory stated that travellers should exercise increased caution because of terrorism threats. On my first trip, I stayed in a hotel, but on my second trip, my colleagues and I stayed two nights in a gated staff compound. I had a 1,000 sq. feet 2-bedroom house to myself—that was a first! Also, for the first time in my travels, I had a security official who spent half an hour with me going through the country's security history and current situation. He also showed me the "safe" room which was within the house—how cool is that! I was told that in the event of a lockdown, I was to take water, food, my phone, and a charger to the room, bolt it, put the phone to silent mode, stay quiet and be prepared to wait for at least two hours whilst the situation was attended to. The door of the safe room was apparently fire and firearm proof. To be clear, at no point in that trip did I feel unsafe, and in fact, it was very reassuring to see the security coverage accorded to the team.

Ironically, the only occasion when I had feared for my safety was when I was in Houston, during a taxi ride from the office to the airport. I was travelling alone and had not arranged for private transportation as I normally would in most countries, as I was told it would be easy and safe to hail a public taxi at the taxi stand. This young driver drove fast, holding his handphone in one hand and having an animated and loud conversation with his friend whilst steering the wheel with the other hand. According to my company's safety guidelines, I was to ask him to end the call and to concentrate on his driving. I contemplated doing so, but weighed the situation. If he did not take kindly to my request (and to my mind, he looked the type, though I could well be wrong), he may well abandon me at the side lane of the highway, and that would have made the situation worse.

To be honest, I just did not have the guts to instruct him to end that conversation. Instead, I spent the entire journey watching the traffic movements, ready to shout out to warn him if there is an emergency. It was a stressful forty-five minute ride. Given another chance, I would definitely have made the request.

"Safety Is The Number One Rule For A Traveller –Travel Safe And Return Home Safely!"

Treat fire alarms with seriousness – evacuate immediately!

First thing to check upon entry to room – evacuation route.

Chapter 5

Travelling Alone

"Alone In This Big, Big, World."

I am not someone you would call an independent traveller. For one, I like to have company. I am also poor with direction and can get lost easily (as an example, on one trip, my husband took out the map and pointed out where we were to go. I said 'ok, let's go'. I proceeded to step forward in one direction whilst he stepped off in the opposite direction). I also often look to others for ideas on what to do on a holiday, as I am usually too lazy or indecisive to make any travel decisions on my own.

Hence, business travel was at first an unnerving experience, as for many of these trips, I would be the only one flying out from Singapore. I used to dread the process - packing for the trip, going to the airport, getting on the plane, sitting through the flight, arriving at the destination, queuing to clear immigration, finding transportation from the airport to hotel, checking in, and finally going into my room and sitting alone on the bed. I would count the hours and days before I could make my way back home, and knowing that to do so, I would have to go through the entire process again.

In my early days of travelling, I once called a friend from the airport, looking for some reassuring words of support before I got on the plane. I even shed some silent tears whilst talking to her, such was the stress and anxiety of flying alone. I then called my mum to report that I had arrived at the airport and was about to get on the plane, but I did not share my feelings with her, as one does not share such feelings with parents—we do not want them to worry about us. Well, the calls helped to calm my nerves, and the trip went well, but it showed how one can get stressed by an overseas trip.

I also dreaded having to eat alone in a foreign land. You go into a restaurant, gesture for a table for one, order your food and, well, wait for your food. I often brought along a newspaper to pass the time or played games on my phone (no WhatsApp/Facebook/Instagram in those days), or simply indulged in people watching (which can be interesting, actually).

That was many years ago. Somewhere down the line, I began to ease up and started to enjoy the experience. Travelling alone has its benefits. It has helped me to be more street smart. I learned to be alert and careful, to keep my wits around me, to be spontaneous and calm when things did not go according to plan, and to open up to strangers. I still get lost sometimes (or most times) but even then, it is interesting to have an unplanned experience and discover new things along the way.

Travelling alone also provides me with a lot more 'me' time than I can have at home in Singapore. I used the time to work, ponder on some areas of life, dream about holidays, or simply observe my surroundings, which often triggers new thoughts in my head.

It has also enabled me to cross paths briefly with many other travellers.

I recall an occasion when a restaurant "assigned" a dining partner to me. This can only happen in a Chinese restaurant, and this time, I was in London's Chinatown. The waiter beckoned to me and a Chinese guy and asked if we would be agreeable to share a table. We looked at one another and said yes, as saying no would mean a longer waiting time on a packed weekday evening. It was awkward initially, as it reminded me of a blind dinner date. It was when our dishes arrived that we started chatting. We both chuckled when we realized we had ordered similar dishes and could have saved money and food if we had combined orders. That started the conversation, and we spent an enjoyable hour eating and chatting about our jobs, football (he was impressed by my knowledge of EPL and Liverpool Football Club), comparing London and Manchester (he lived in Manchester), how we met our spouses, etc. Having a dining partner certainly made the food tastier! Our paths never crossed again, but for that hour or so, it was a fulfilling and interesting experience to enjoy dinner with a stranger.

I also remembered the time I was waiting in the transit lounge for my connecting flight to Canada. It was a rather long wait. I had already travelled for almost 15 hours and was feeling worn out (the trip took 27 hours door-to-door and has remained the longest non-stop journey I have ever taken.) I still struck a conversation with a Caucasian lady sitting next to me who was reading a book. She shared that she was a missionary. It was interesting to hear about her life story and her work. It also got me thinking about my life, how I could contribute to society, and about my passions. I cannot recall the fine details of our conversation, but I remember distinctly that at one point in our conversation, she looked at me and asked me earnestly if I was married. Her question surprised me and I replied "no, I have not found the one yet." She then said sincerely that it was very important that I find a life partner to share my life with, and to pray for one. I often think back at this encounter and wondered why a stranger would say such things. Perhaps she was carrying a message from God, and yes, I held her advice close to my heart.

Then there was this young Indian lady in her early 20s who sat next to me on a flight from the UK to Singapore. We started chatting after I showed her how to recline her seat (it was the first time she was travelling in a business class cabin). She shared that she had just completed her studies and was excited about getting a job. She was thinking of joining the UN to 'help the world'. It was refreshing to see someone young and full of dreams, and I felt envious as I bemoaned the loss of my youth. She also shared that she was going to a beach resort in Sri Lanka to spend Christmas and was looking forward to catching up with family and having a sunny Christmas. Two weeks later, I read about the Indonesia earthquake and tsunamis that hit several countries, including Sri Lanka. She came to my mind immediately, and I prayed for her safety. Hopefully, she is now somewhere in the world, fulfilling her dream as a UN official.

On another occasion, I struck up a brief conversation with an old lady who was returning home to the UK after a trip to New Zealand. I could tell that she was proud of her son, and rightly so, as she shared that her son had bought her a business class ticket to ensure her comfort on a long flight, and that she appreciated it as she could indeed rest well on the flight. As I walked out of the arrival hall, I saw her being greeted by her son, who came with an enormous bouquet of flowers and gave her a bear hug. That really warmed my heart. She must have brought up her son well to have such a loving relationship with him. This was a good reminder to be filial to my parents!

Then there was this elderly British gentleman who sat next to me in economy class on a flight from Singapore to Manchester. I was heading there to attend a funeral—not the happiest of occasions. He was travelling home after visiting his brother in Australia. He appeared to have some difficulty in walking, and I felt sorry that he was seated right at the end of the plane. We engaged in some small talk. He was a World War II veteran and had gone to visit his brother, who was ill. This may be the last time he saw his brother, he shared. "I am too old to travel such a long distance," he said. I felt sorry for what he had just said, as I knew in my heart he was probably right. He then went to the toilet and took a long time, which got me worried. When he came back, he told me with fear in his eyes, "I had blood on my stool!" That really got me worried. I tried to reassure him by saying that he probably had not drunk enough water and was dehydrated, so I went to the flight attendant to get him a drink. He drank and managed to get some sleep for the rest of the journey. I wished him well!

I even got a 'job offer' once on a flight to London! It was a morning flight, and I used the bulk of the 13-hour journey working on my laptop. Several hours into the flight, an elderly gentleman walked past my seat, and we smiled at one another. He suddenly remarked, "I want to hire you for my company! You've been working non-stop since we got on this flight!" I laughed and had a brief chat with him, but later kicked myself for not taking the opportunity to "network" and at least exchanged name cards.

And then there's Kate (see "Kate's Adventure"), and in another chapter, I will share about the time I missed my flight and spent the night with a stranger!

Travelling alone can be boring, but it is encounters like these that make the experiences memorable.

"Travelling Alone Can Be Refreshing And Enlightening!"

Keep your wits around you but be open to interact with strangers. You never know what you can learn from them.

Chapter 6

Kate's Adventure & The Pillars of Life

It was 2007, and I was on a Singapore Airlines flight from London to Singapore, having spent two weeks in London. The Business Class section in those days was unlike those in today's planes, which offer more privacy. It used to have two passengers sitting side by side, albeit with the same roomy and comfortable seats of today.

On my right, seated on the window seat, was an elderly British lady who looked like she might be in her late 70s. A frail figure, she was well dressed and had a sweet smile, with kind wrinkled eyes and a full head of white hair. I sensed a sweet, faint aroma of lavender around her. We did not talk initially, apart from the usual courtesy nod that two strangers trapped in a 14-hour flight would give one another.

We started engaging in small talk when our meals were served. Her name was Katherine, and this was the first time she was flying on her own. It was her first time in a Business Class cabin, too. Katherine's destination was New Zealand, where she would spend three months with her daughter. As we chatted, she began to share more.

Kate ("call me Kate") and her husband John used to own a bed and breakfast in Surrey. They ran it for over fifteen years, but she had sold it some months before, after the passing of John the year before. "After he left, I wanted to continue running the business. But it was difficult to manage the place all by myself, and I also lost my heart for it and found it meaningless to run the business without him. It just wasn't the same." She gave a shy smile and continued, "there were too many memories of him and us around the house. Anyway, I sold it at a good price. I had not realized it was worth quite a lot of money!"

Her eyes glanced away, and I could tell she was thinking of John at that moment. "He really loved running the inn. We had customers from all over the world, even Singapore!" Then, suddenly, the smile disappeared, and she became subdued. "But it's all over now. I had surgery on my back six months ago and was in the hospital for three months. My daughter persuaded me to sell the place and to go stay with her for a few months. Then I will decide what to do and where to live next. I'm homeless now, do you know?" She chuckled a little at the word "homeless."

It was a long journey from London to New Zealand—over 24 hours, and I was concerned whether she would be up to it, especially given that she had just recovered from back surgery. I then asked if she was feeling alright so far, as she still had quite a distance to go before reaching her destination.

"Twenty-four hours? Is it going to be that long? Oh my God, I did not know that! What was I thinking of! I really should not have made this trip!" A tear suddenly appeared on her cheeks. I was angry with myself and gave myself a mental slap for getting her worried and quickly assured her that everything was going to be ok and that she could stay at my place if she felt she needed to rest before the Singapore-New Zealand leg.

Thankfully, she calmed down and even managed to catch a nap. Before the plane touched down, I checked on her again, and she assured me that she was fine. I waited with her as the passengers got off the plane. When the flight attendant came to help the elderly passengers with mobility issues to disembark, I asked the flight attendant to take good care of her.

"I'm ok, don't you worry!" Kate assured me again. "Enjoy New Zealand, Kate, and God bless you," I wished her. "Thank you, thank you. I will, I will. God bless you too!"

I was reminded of my brief encounter with Kate when I watched the movie *Up* a few years later. I felt a lump in my throat and a tear in my eye (and they said it was a "cartoon" movie) during the segment in which Carl sat on his chair, looking at the empty chair where Ellie used to sit next to him, and wondered what to do next.

When a spouse passes on, the absence may leave a void that is difficult to fill for the spouse left behind. This is particularly so if the couple had been together for many years and had a close, loving relationship, doing everything together—meals, long walks, shopping, holidays, daily conversations, building an unbreakable bond over the years.

On the one hand, it is sweet to do everything with your soulmate and keep the relationship strong and growing, but I realised it is also important to have your own separate dreams and goals. Try out new things alone, maintaining your personal relationships with friends and family, and not live life with your spouse with him or her as the only focus, as you may risk losing the reason or motivation for your existence when your other half departs.

As Ellie wrote to Carl, "Thanks for the adventure. Now go and have a new one. Love, Ellie".

Carl found his adventure, and the will to carry on. So will Kate, I believe!

Are You Standing on Strong Pillars?

This encounter also reminded me of the concept of the "Pillars of a Fulfilling and Happy Life." Google "pillars of life" and you will find a handful of articles relating to this[12] [13]. It basically encourages one to live life strongly, rooted in a robust and balanced foundation, and based on a few areas that are key to our life. Based on the readings, I have summarised them into: **Soul** (spiritual and personal growth), **Heart** (relationships and bonds), **Body** (physical and mental health), **Mind** (goals and sense of purpose), **Wealth** (financial and time freedom).

Each area may require different levels of priority and focus from us at different points in our lives, but what is key is that we remain in sync and in control at all times and not lose the balance, otherwise, we may "lose" ourselves as a result.

- **Soul**: A lifelong, continual process of understanding and development to become a better version of ourselves by applying our spiritual beliefs. Some may see this as pursuing the philosophical meaning of life and existence. No one is perfect and searching inward into our souls enables us to acknowledge what we can do to be a better person, son or daughter, spouse, friend, neighbour, colleague, citizen. Cultivate a strong bond with your soul, and you will never be lost or feel empty.
- **Heart**: We yearn to feel loved and cherished. We want to have a sense of belonging; with our family who gives us unconditional love and support, with friends who will walk through thick and thin with us and share common interests and even dreams, with colleagues whom we spend at least 8 hours with daily, and with our soul mate (if we have one) who accepts and loves us, warts and all,

and with whom we made a vow—to have and to hold, for better, for worse, for richer, for poorer, in sickness and in health, till death do us part. All relationships are special but, like everything else, they need TLC (tender loving care). The memories and love you grow in your heart for them are what makes life worth living, I feel.

· **Body**: Everyone knows the value of a healthy body and mind, but we sometimes forget why 'health is wealth', especially when we are young and able and there are other priorities to focus on. The "remediation" in later years for a neglected body can be expensive and painful.

· **Mind**: The human mind is engineered to think and act. Having a goal gives us purpose and keeps us going. For some, climbing the career ladder is their primary goal. Through our work, we also pick up new, varied experiences and knowledge, and that is great for our development. That said, pursuing a career should not be our sole purpose in life, for you may risk losing your identity when you step off the career path. Set other new goals and challenges from time to time and continually seek new knowledge. I learned about getting out of my comfort zone many years ago, and it has challenged and served me well. I love the saying, *"If you always do what you've always done, you always get what you've always gotten."*[14] That realisation has led me to new goals and paths, new experiences, fun and fear, sometimes all at the same time!

· **Wealth**: Like it or not, we need to accumulate enough assets to afford financial and time freedom. Unless we have wealthy parents or have received a neat inheritance, we must earn our keep through our savings and investments. I am responsible for my financial health, and that means making decisions, improving my investment knowledge, and being clear on the level of risk I am prepared to take. Some executives are so busy at work that their finances are neglected, either through imprudent spending or simply leaving cash in savings accounts that earn peanuts. Then there is the question of how much one needs to retire comfortably. That is never an easy one to answer, but the earlier you think and act on it, the better. Discipline in wealth management is a prerequisite to financial freedom, but this is also where many of us fare poorly in.

The busy executive who is chasing his career goals and going on multiple business trips may struggle with or neglect the other pillars of his life. No one is indispensable at work, but we are indispensable to our families and loved ones. As the saying goes, no one on their deathbed ever said, "I wish I had worked more!"

In the book The Top Five Regrets of the Dying, Bronnie Ware[15], a palliative nurse, shared the most common regrets of her patients:

1. I wish I'd had the courage to live a life true to myself, not the life others expected of me.
2. I wish I didn't work so hard.
3. I wish I'd had the courage to express my feelings.
4. I wish I had stayed in touch with my friends.
5. I wish I had let myself be happier.

You may notice that each of the five regrets can be linked to one of the pillars of life above. Food for thought!

No matter your age, keep learning, and keep going on new adventures!

Ensure the pillars of your life are robust and balanced despite your busy career and business trips. Take stock and do a self-assessment on the sturdiness of your pillars annually.

Chapter 7

Stranger for a Roommate

*"Angels Appear When We Least Expect Them, And When
We Need Them The Most."*

The year was 2004, and I was on my first business trip to Houston, flying via Los Angeles (there were no direct flights in those days), to attend my first team meeting for a new position I was taking up the next month. I was excited but nervous about what to expect for the long trip and if I would be able to click with the new team.

The journey there was smooth. I flew from Singapore to Los Angeles(LA), followed by an overnight airport hotel stay, and then hopped onto a domestic flight to Houston the next morning. Queuing up at the Houston immigration counter (it was always a long wait), I struck up a conversation with a Chinese guy, who turned out to be a Singaporean. What is more, we discovered we both worked for the same company, but in different lines of Businesses! Talk about coincidences.

As we chatted, he asked if I had brought a phone with me. "No," I replied. The US had a different telecommunications standard from ours in those days, so there was no point in bringing my phone, and I had not asked for a company loaned US phone either. "I'm only here for a few days, so it should not be an issue," I told him. He raised his eyebrows and seemed somewhat concerned. He then whipped out an international phone card to give to me, saying that I could use it in case of an emergency. I tried to reject it initially, but then accepted his gift. As things turned out, I ended up needing the card!

The two-and-a-half-days meeting went supremely well, and despite being the newcomer, everyone made me feel welcomed and a part of the team, which I appreciated. The meeting ended slightly earlier, and we left promptly to make the homeward journey. What a successful trip this had been, I was thinking to myself, and I felt very good then.

I did not foresee what was coming. The check-in process for the return leg was relatively smooth, and I then sat in a corner waiting for my domestic flight back to LA. I even dozed off for a few minutes! When I awoke, I noticed that the departure time for my flight (and many other flights) had been pushed back. And then it got pushed further back. My connecting flight from LA to Singapore was to depart at 10 pm, so the delay left me with less and less time to be on time to catch the connecting flight.

I started to panic and asked the counter staff for some information. "Bad weather in the region, so all flights are being pushed back," she explained.

For a few stressful hours, I paced the terminal floors, praying that the weather would improve. Being a relatively young and inexperienced traveller then, I did not quite know what to do. I soon gave up hope of catching the 10 pm flight but hoped that SQ would put me on the next flight at 1 am. I used the card to call my family and Singapore Airlines. It was soothing to speak to someone in such distressing times, so I was glad I had the card.

At around 8 pm or so we finally boarded the plane. I was seated in Economy Class, with a Chinese girl on my left and a Caucasian chap on my right. All three of us were roughly of the same age range. By then, I was mentally and physically exhausted. The plane took a long time to depart and when it finally started pushing back from the terminal gate, I relaxed and closed my eyes. All sorted, I thought. I then dozed off.

When I woke up some minutes later, I realized we were still on the ground! "What happened? Why are we still here?" I asked the girl on my left. "Well, the pilot went to the runway and came back to the gate as clearance was not given."

"WTF!" was my involuntary immediate reaction. Well, the girl did better than me and went on a rant. She then shared that she was heading to LA simply to pick up her parents at the airport and to take the return leg back to Houston with them. She was worried about them flying alone as they could not speak English and had decided it would be best that she picked them up personally from the LA airport. I was touched by her filial piety. She must have been feeling very worried, and I imagined her parents standing somewhere at the airport waiting anxiously for her to show up, and not knowing what was happening.

By now I was wide awake, but with nothing to do or read. The guy on my right was playing games on a handheld console. Maybe I was peeking too much; he suddenly turned to me and asked if I would like to give it a go. Embarrassed, I declined. "No, it's ok!" he insisted. I sucked at playing games anyway, so I declined again. But it felt good to be sitting between two caring souls. I then closed my eyes and went to dreamland again.

We eventually arrived in LA, but all flights from LA to Singapore had departed. To make matters worse, the sole of one of my shoes cracked, and I had to dig out my work heels from my suitcase (a case of Murphy's law?). I managed to find the Singapore Airlines counter, which was jam-packed with similar travellers who had missed their flights. Thankfully, I managed to get a replacement ticket for the next evening. By then it was after 2 am.

I was about to leave the counter when a middle-aged Chinese lady came up to me and asked in Mandarin if I could speak Mandarin. She was so relieved to know that I could and then sought my help to communicate with the counter staff to get a replacement ticket for her flight to Taiwan. She also managed to get one for the next evening.

I then asked her what she was going to do next. She replied that as she could not speak English, there was nothing much she could do by herself. She would just find a place to rest at the airport and spend the next day roaming the airport.

There was no way I was going to leave her there by herself. I then asked if she would like to join me in finding a hotel to stay for the night. Her eyes brightened up, and she seemed quite relieved to hear this and accepted my offer immediately, thanking me profusely.

In those days, there was a wall panel at the airport that showed a list of the different hotels near the airport, and all you needed to do was to pick up the phone at the panel and press the number assigned to the hotel. I was not expecting any issue in getting a hotel room. I started calling the 5-star hotels. There was no room available! I then tried the 4-star hotels, and finally the 3-star hotels, after I could not get any room anywhere else. From one of the calls, I understood that there was a major convention in town, hence most hotels were packed. I could not believe my luck (Murphy's law again?). I then called the 3-star motels, and finally struck lottery with one which was the second last hotel on the list, and with one last room available. What a relief! The motel then sent a driver to pick us up, which came 30 minutes later. Going through the quiet and dark streets at this hour, with a stranger for a driver, and a new acquaintance next to me, I admit I was feeling rather frightened and worried. Was I grateful then that I was not alone, and that I had my new friend's company!

It was after 3 am when we arrived at the motel. I was pleased to see the place looked decent. Upon entering our room, I bolted the door immediately and then checked out the room thoroughly. All was good - the beds looked clean, and the room seemed well kept. Motels are as good as hotels, I realised. I then used the calling card to call my parents to convey the turn of events. I then passed the card to her to call her husband, which she thanked me for, and said she was very grateful to have me with her.

"Aunty" (as I called her—this is a Singaporean trait; we address strangers who are older than us as "Aunty" or "Uncle") had spent the last few weeks with her sister, who lived in San Diego with her American husband. Her husband was not able to join her on this trip as he could not take the time off (they ran a small printing business back home). She too, had missed her connecting flight because of bad weather, and she thanked me again for taking care of her. I told her I was actually very happy to have her company, as I would otherwise be all alone!

With this turn of events, this new "mother and daughter" team then went to bed, and we spent the next 20 hours or so together. We had a good breakfast the next morning, and after checking out of the hotel, we did the next best thing I could think of to occupy our time—a day tour of LA! Before getting on the tour, I bought a pair of flip-flops from the supermarket as there was no way I could walk the whole day in my work heels.

It was a sunny day, and the tour took us to various tourist hot spots, including checking out the homes of some celebrities, and we had a pleasant lunch under the sun at an alfresco restaurant. It was a totally relaxing day, which helped to erase the stress of the day before.

We then made the return trip to the airport. This time, everything went smoothly. I invited Aunty to join me in the lounge and we had a nice relaxing dinner. My flight time was earlier than hers. Before we parted ways, she gave me a note with her name and contact details. "If you ever go to Taipei, you must come and look for me!"

I thanked her for her company, and she said the same. We had a bear hug, and I then left for the gate. We never met again. (It was a long while before I would make a trip to Taipei, but by then I had forgotten her offer. It would have been nice to have a reunion!)

When I look back at this eventful trip, one thing was evident to me. God looks out and takes care of us. That explained the phone card which I received, and for Aunty and me to have each other for company. Amen!

SHARING TIP!

Ensure you always have a phone with you. You never know when an emergency comes up.

Make the best out of an unplanned event. Stressing yourself out does not change the situation.

Chapter 8

A Hurricane Trip

"It Pays To Travel Light."

After the eventful trip in 2004 (see "Stranger for a room-mate"), I was pleased that the following year's leadership team meeting would be held in Singapore and that I would host the team. No twenty-hour flight to take, I get to keep the comfort of my bed, and most of all, my team and I would have the chance to introduce Singapore and our plant (I was working at a production plant) to colleagues from other parts of the world.

However, about one and a half months before the meeting was to take place, in late August, Hurricane Katrina struck. It was a Category Five cyclone and one of the most destructive hurricanes ever to hit the United States, causing thousands of deaths, flooding, and leaving millions homeless along the Gulf Coast and in New Orleans[16]. It was heartbreaking to see the destruction that it wrought. Some of the leadership team members were from Houston. One lost his holiday home, whilst the houses of two others were badly affected by the hurricane's passing force.

A week later, my boss decided we would still go ahead with the meeting, but the location would be moved from Singapore to Houston, to minimize travel for the American colleagues, and allow them the flexibility to take care of their personal affairs as needed. I was disappointed, of course, but I understood his decision.

And so, in mid-September, I made my way to Houston again and arrived safely, with no hiccups. The office building where our meeting was to be held was in town, and on the way there, one could see that the city was in recovery mode, with debris along the streets. I also passed by the indoor stadium, the Astrodome, where many evacuees had gone to seek shelter. It was clear it would take months, if not years, for the city and the region to recover fully from the damage that Katrina had brought about.

It was good to catch up with my colleagues, to see how they were faring, and to hear "Katrina stories" from our American colleagues. I brought a mooncake as it was the mid-autumn festival period, and we had a Chinese tea with mooncake (a traditional Chinese pastry) appreciation session, allowing me to share a piece of the original plan for the rescinded Singapore meeting. Eating mooncakes is a symbol of a reunion, and it felt nice to have this mini celebration together after a year apart.

Unfortunately, drama developed on Day 2. We heard in the Morning News that a new hurricane, Rita, might approach Texas' shores. This was confirmed after lunch, and all meetings were cancelled immediately. Staff were told to make their way home.

I could not believe this was happening. My flight reservation was for the late afternoon of the following day, but I needed to fly out now. Most of my colleagues who flew in had no issues in getting their tickets, as they were taking a direct international flight, but not me, as I had to take a domestic flight out of Houston to Los Angeles. My Travel Desk was closed because of the time difference between the US and Singapore. The Travel Desk in the US could not help me much either, other than to say, "You are unlikely to get a ticket today. Why don't you try at the Airport Ticketing Office, but no promises! I suggest you try again tomorrow morning."

With no assurance of a domestic flight ticket back to Los Angeles, my colleagues advised me to check into an airport hotel and to make my way to the airport early the next morning. That seemed the most practical thing to do. On the way to the airport hotel, we saw long rows of cars making their way out of the city. Tension was in the air. (With memories of Katrina still fresh in everyone's mind, Hurricane Rita became the largest evacuation of people in United States history, and resulted in many deaths on the freeways, including a bus with elderly evacuees onboard, which had caught fire on a Texas highway.[17])

I checked into the Hilton Airport Hotel alone. The hotel was eerily quiet. Dinner was a sad affair at the hotel restaurant, with only two other tables occupied by diners. Everyone's eyes were glued to the TV screen, with the newscasters giving continual updates on the hurricane and the evacuation situation.

I tried to distract myself by doing some work in the evening, but it was difficult, not least because I could hear the regular streams of horn-honking from cars, sirens from police cars, and as every TV channel I switched on only talked about Rita and showed Americans preparing for the hurricane. To top things off, at around midnight, a slip of paper came through my door. It said that due to the hurricane, the hotel would cease operations at 7 am and requested all guests to check out by then.

Well, if I were not panicking yet, I would be after reading that note. I could not sleep much that night, and throughout the night, the constant din of horns and sirens from the vehicles on the road blasted into my room. It was scary and distressing, to say the least!

I got out of bed and checked out of the hotel at 5 am. Please, allow me to make a confession here. For the first time in my life, I stole something—a bottle of water and a bar of chocolate from the fridge bar. I was sorry I did not pay for them as there were no staff at the checkout counter when I came down, but I was glad I had them with me later. (See also Appendix, Tip #2—always bring snacks with you on a trip!)

A few other guests were at the lobby with the same intention—to make sure we could get on the first hotel bus to the airport. By 5:15 am, we were on our way. Upon arrival ten minutes later, I saw that it was total chaos everywhere. There were massive crowds, young and old, invalids and able-bodied, spread all over the terminal check-in areas, and everyone had the same aim—to get on a flight before all flights ceased.

I felt rather upset seeing elderly folk, especially those with mobility issues, jostling for space amidst the crowd of younger and stronger bodies. One Chinese gentleman was in a wheelchair with presumably his granddaughter wheeling him and struggling to manage her luggage at the same time. Then there were families with young kids, some too young to walk by themselves and had to be carried by exhausted looking parents. Others came with no luggage, just a small weekend bag. Everyone looked distressed and worried—it was a rather heart-wrenching moment for me, for I felt we were like refugees, scrambling to be evacuated from a dangerous zone.

I also quickly realized that the airport was thinly staffed, with most counters not manned, and leaving the brave few who turned up for duty totally swarmed. Queues formed everywhere, but one did not know what the different queues were for. I had to change a few queue lines before I found the right line. I was relieved that I only had a cabin-sized bag with me and did not need to check in any luggage, for that would be looking at yet another much longer queue. (That's another tip in the Appendix–always travel light).

After some nerve wrecking minutes, I managed to get my ticket for the originally scheduled flight time. I was so relieved to hold the ticket and said a hearty thanks to the brave lady who was manning the counter. I then sped off to join the queue for security clearance and then entered the departure terminal hall. Another problem then arose. The flight information panel was not active, and there was no way of knowing which gate was for which flight. I had intended to go to the gate for the next available flight to Los Angeles to try my luck and see if they would let me get a seat on an earlier flight. I scrambled from gate to gate, asking any airport personnel I could find for help. By sheer luck, I found it after a couple of minutes, and I could also change my ticket to the morning flight! Only at that point did my heartbeat slow down a notch, and I was able to relax a little.

The plane flew out successfully, though it was delayed by several minutes as the pilot wanted to get as many people on board as possible. I subsequently read that many people who had tickets were unable to get on their planes that day due to the high influx of people. Many could not even get through the entrance to the airport.

This was certainly a most stressful experience, perhaps surpassing the previous year's experience, but looking back, it was an exciting chapter of my business travel life, and through such experiences, one gets a notch wiser on travelling dos and don'ts.

It would be years later before I would go on another trip to Houston. History repeated itself again, and I was stuck at the Los Angeles Airport for the afternoon with a delayed flight. Thankfully, I was not alone on that trip. My colleague said her Houston trips had always been smooth until this trip, and she said in jest that I must have caused this delay. I could not defend myself. Nevertheless, we had a good time chatting away, window shopping, and having a wonderful lunch at the airport.

SHARING TIP!

Always travel light where possible, using a cabin sized bag. This forces you to pack light. It also helps you to zip in and out of airport quickly, saving time.

Chapter 9

Of Missing Trains
and Flights

"Mind The Gap!"

The London public transport system is brilliant when it works, but when there are issues—system failures, strikes, weather disruption, etc—the entire city turns upside down and frustration, pain, grief, and anger overcome disgruntled travellers.

That is what happened one October day in 2017, when I needed to travel to Heathrow Airport to take a flight to attend a board meeting in China. I had planned to take a tube ride from my place in central London to Paddington Station and then get on the Heathrow Express train to the airport. Just as I had done numerous times before, when I do not plan to take a cab to the airport. On this occasion, I could not have taken a cab anyway as the M4 highway was closed, so the tube route was still the best.

I knew that there were some transport issues because of an ongoing strike, but only realized after arriving at the station that the tube service for my route was not working that day. "Argh, why do things not go my way when I am in a rush!" I muttered to myself.

I rushed out of the station, and by sheer luck managed to hail a cab promptly. I told the driver to go to Paddington Station and to be fast but safe, as I needed to catch a train that was running on reduced frequency.

To his credit, he manoeuvred through some side streets and roads that I had never known before and got me to the station with five minutes to spare. I rushed to the platform, tugging along my cabin bag and haversack. The station was jam packed with people and so was the Heathrow Express train. I went from compartment to compartment looking for a space to squeeze into, but had no luck.

Walking back (or perhaps I was pacing a bit, but I was not running) from the tail end of the train to take another look, my left leg suddenly went dead and became "locked", causing me to fall. I do not know how this happened, but somehow my legs fell into the gap between the train and the platform, with my hands holding on to the edges of the platform! This was yet another embarrassing moment in my life, and dozens of pairs of eyes in the train compartment nearest to me were now staring at my miserable situation. A station staff came up to me immediately and helped me up, but instead of asking how I was, he berated me for rushing and said I could have waited for the next train (frequency–30 minutes).

I tried to defend myself but got no sympathy. That said, suddenly, enough space opened in the compartment nearest to me (the magic of sympathy!) and I managed to get in. By then I was drenched in sweat, one arm of my jacket was slightly ripped, and my cabin bag had acquired a few "Paddington battle" scratches.

Looking back, the station staff was right in that there was no need to panic, as I could have taken the next train. I usually plan to get to the airport early, hence I had some buffer time to spare. But, somehow, the fact that things were not running per MY PLAN ruffled my composure. It is the "things are supposed to go as planned in THIS way, and NOT any other way" mentality.

This reminds me of another trip, also on the Heathrow Express to the airport (there is a third story, in which my husband, holding our train tickets, ran and hopped onto the train and the door closed before I got on, but let's focus on this story first). It was a smooth ride, but 5 minutes before reaching the airport, the train suddenly stopped. I was calm initially, but the wait became 15 minutes, then 30 minutes, and all this while the train remained at a standstill. My time buffer was fast being breached, and we had a plane to catch!

I turned to my husband. "OMG, we are going to miss our flight. What should we do!" My voice was clearly agitated and turning panicky. "We can only wait. What can we do anyway? Just chill," was his unimpassioned reply. I was amazed at his calmness. Looking around our compartment, I realized that other than me, everyone else kept a calm composure. Most just sat there silently and waited or continued to play with their phones or read their books. A few picked up their phones to make some calls, but everyone had an aura of calm around them. Was this a manifestation of the British "Keep Calm and Carry on" mentality?

At that moment, it dawned on me that was the right way to respond to situations outside of our control. A calm mind makes the best decisions and getting stressed gets you nowhere. That everyone kept calm also helped me to cool down quickly.

We missed our flight to Austria but managed to get on the next flight which was departing only two hours later (an advantage of flying with national airlines—there are usually several flights per day!), so we missed little of our holiday.

Reflecting on this and earlier chapters, I could not help but wonder why, after all these experiences, I have not managed to learn to keep my cool when things do not go according to plan when it relates to time and schedules. Is this some obsession of mine with needing to keep to the timetable? Something for me to reflect on.

As for that third story, I got on the next train, and thankfully, as I had a soft copy of the train tickets on my phone, I did not have any issues with the conductor. I gave my sheepish looking husband my best 'how could you leave me behind' glare when he met me at Heathrow Airport. We had a good laugh over it.

"Keep Calm. Getting Stressed Only Increases One's Heart Rate But Achieves Nothing Else."

Follow the British. Keep calm and do not worry. Also, 'mind the gap' on the train tracks!

Chapter 10

Taking a Bleisure Trip

"A Trip Like This Is How Friendships Are Made, And Where Memories Of A Lifetime Are Formed."

Wikipedia defines bleisure travel as "the activity of combining business travel with leisure time[18]." Basically, it refers to the business traveller extending the duration of their business trip to enjoy some sightseeing and other leisure activities. Apparently, this phenomenon has been studied since 2011, and it has seen a constant growth in recent years[19].

My very first business trip in 1993 was a de facto bleisure trip, though the term had not been coined then. Fresh out of school, I joined Arthur Andersen (AA) as a tax consultant a month after my last final exam paper. One of the perks of joining AA was the two-week induction course at the Centre for Professional Education, at St Charles in Chicago, which provides rigorous formal training to all recruits and the opportunity to bond and build the AA culture for the participants coming from different parts of the world[20].

This course was the highlight of the first year for all recruits, and everyone had the same plan—to attend the course and then scoot off on a few weeks' vacation in the United States. We attended the course in different batches and each batch would make its own travel plans. I was in the October batch, and my group comprised two guys and two girls.

Until then, I had not been on any flights that lasted over four hours. One colleague had never even been on a plane before, and this was her first ever flight! This was thus a trip of many "firsts" for me—my first intercontinental trip, my first trip to the United States, my first overseas course, the first time I would be out of Singapore for a month, and the first time I was travelling with people whom I had only known for a few months.

We got on an early morning United Airlines flight and flew for eight hours to Tokyo, where we had a three-hour layover, followed by a ten-hour flight before finally arriving in Chicago. It was amusing to note that after all this travelling, we touched down at 2 pm US time on the same day that we had left Singapore many hours before!

The two-week training course went by quickly, and we had a thoroughly splendid time. St Charles was an impressive training campus with vast grounds, pleasant rooms (each shared by two students), canteens, and many other facilities. We had come at the right season too—beautiful autumn, when the air was cold and there was mist and ice on some mornings (I learned the hard way that one should not try to sweep ice off from a bench!), and to top it off, beautiful grounds where autumn leaves were beginning to fall, leaving a luxurious mix of red and yellow colours on the ground and a romantic feel in the air. The grounds also played host to many wild animals—I saw hares, squirrels, chipmunks, and racoons.

Each class had students from different parts of the world—Hong Kong, Switzerland, Malaysia, France, Germany, and from different states within the United States. I had not had the chance to study abroad or to live on a university campus, so this was the closest I had to an overseas education experience, and I relished the opportunity. (Arthur Andersen may have folded amidst the Enron scandal, but it continued to hold a special spot in my heart, as my first employer, and for the opportunities and friendships it gave me.)

It was fun to live and study with people from other countries. I looked forward to the daily lessons and activities. Besides the classes and assessments, there were daily evening activities (e.g., snooker, volleyball, ping pong, bar games). We learned more about the different countries and cultures, and it also gave us the opportunity to share more about Singapore (such as correcting a colleague who thought Singapore was a part of China).

It was also great that the four of us bonded particularly well, and at some point, we must have crossed the line from being colleagues to becoming good friends. By the time we left St Charles to embark on our two-week trip, we were well acquainted with each other's quirks and personalities.

We started off by travelling to Toronto, then New York, Orlando, Las Vegas, with San Francisco as our last stop. Our budget was tight as we had only started working some months before, so we stayed in budget hotels and where allowable, the four of us even squeezed into one room which had two beds. I recalled that there was even one night in which three of us shared a bed, whilst the fourth spent the night with a relative. Such was our determination to spend as little as possible! Our budget for each meal was less than $10, and so we ate a lot of meals from MacDonald's, cheap Chinese eateries, and pizza joints.

When writing this chapter, I re-read my diary entries for this trip and shared some of them with the three colleagues I had travelled with. We had a good laugh reminiscing over some of the interesting incidents and the hotels we had stayed in, dug out from the recesses of memories from 28 years ago!

The best word I could use to summarise that trip is "eye-opener." As a young 22-year-old, the trip exposed me to the world outside of Singapore, and I was no longer "the frog in the well".

The things that our eyes saw and soaked in (e.g. one can never forget the majesty of Niagara falls), the different sounds that our ears heard (e.g. pay-out sounds from the casino slot machines, though unfortunately, they were not from the machines we played on), the sights that triggered emotional responses in the heart (such as seeing homeless people who were unsheltered. On our last night in San Francisco, we gave all our loose change to a young homeless mother who was out on the streets with her child), the streets that our feet trod on (we were bewildered to see steam pouring from New York roads), the people from all races that our hands shook (including that of Mickey and Minnie Mouse), and the different foods that we ate (to be honest, our meals were mostly average quality stuff, but I recalled we had a sumptuous yet inexpensive dim sum meal in San Francisco. We had joined a long queue line outside the restaurant without knowing what it was offering–typical Singaporean trait, but it paid off!). All these became very special memories for me to keep and hold. That trip taught me that the world was indeed my oyster, and that there was much to learn by allowing myself to broaden my horizons.

It was many years after that trip that I would take another bleisure trip with colleagues. Time was the biggest challenge — with all the things that needed to be done at home and at work, it was difficult to fork out time to spend a few days travelling for pleasure after a business trip. Companionship was also an issue—everyone was at that stage of life where we were busy with work and family commitments, and our common goal was to go home immediately after a business trip.

In later years of my career, my husband would sometimes join me on intercontinental trips. It was a practical solution. Since it was difficult for us to plan a holiday in advance given our work commitments and the various business trips, some of which may have a last-minute change of dates, it was easier to latch on to a confirmed business trip and plan to take a week off before or after the business meeting. We are not detailed planners, and it was sufficient for us just to have our flights and hotels booked. The itinerary planning usually took place in the evenings when we were in the hotel room!

In 2018, I had the opportunity to go on a two-day bleisure trip with colleagues for the second time in my working life. There was a team leadership conference in Houston (yes, Houston again!). Four of us from Singapore were attending the conference, and by pure coincidence, another colleague was also going to Houston for a different meeting that week.

The five of us—all girls—hatched a plan to spend the weekend before the conference in San Francisco and Houston. It had been a long time since I went on an all-girls trip, and well, we sure had a blast of a good time!

A girls' trip differs from a couple or family trip. I would not say it is more fun, but I must confess that going on a 'girls only' trip, with girl-talk all day and night, shopping, chatting, eating, sightseeing plus more shopping, is pure great fun. We felt like 18-year-olds once again.

On this trip, we went to Fisherman's Wharf to visit the colony of sea lions (they looked the same as when I had last seen them 25 years before), took the ferry to Sausalito, went on a long walk to the Golden Gate Bridge and took several videos and photos with the bridge as our background. We joined the long queue to jump onto the famous cable cars at night and went to just about every market, shop, and outlet out there. On the food experience front, we had a big breakfast spread, a sumptuous seafood meal and a delicious American-style dinner.

Reflecting on what I had written earlier about my first bleisure trip to the United States, in which our last stop had been San Francisco, it was special to note that my second bleisure trip with colleagues had coincidentally been at the same place where I ended my first bleisure trip!

I also noticed the differences between that trip and the second bleisure trip. In the latter, we stayed in a nice, posh business hotel, and we purposely sought the best restaurants. On my first bleisure trip, we stayed in a $70 per night budget hotel and had budget meals most of the time. What a difference 25 years can bring! I must say, though, the fun was the same.

After many years of solo business travel, it was nice to be travelling with a group of friends who were also colleagues. Good companionship makes a lot of difference to any trip.

SHARING TIP!

Do take a bleisure trip from time to time. Travelling with colleagues turn a colleague into a friend!

Chapter 11

The "Firsts" In Business Travelling

"What Are Your Best "Firsts" experiences in business travel?

Writing this book has made me realise that business travelling has brought many "first-time" experiences into my life. I have written about some of them in previous chapters, and in this chapter, I attempt to capture the rest!

My First time in Business Class Lounge and Cabin

My first business class trip was in 2003-a flight to Perth, for a team meeting (prior to this, most of my travels were regional flights which did not meet my company's criteria of a minimum 4- hour flight duration to qualify for a business class seat. We used to "gripe" about the flight to Hong Kong, which at 3 hours 55 minutes, missed the mark by mere minutes). Since then, I have been on countless more business class flights, but the first one is always the most special. It started with the usage of the business class lounge. When I handed over my plane ticket to the lounge staff to validate my entry, I suddenly felt that this was official–I was a legit business traveller!

Upon entering the lounge, I was taken in by the size of it, the vast variety of food offerings, newspapers, and magazines, and best still, everything was free of charge. One's greedy eyes immediately became bigger than one's stomach–you want to try everything as everything looks delicious!

Then it was time to board the plane. Wow, the luxury of having a separate line and with early boarding arrangements –

it makes one feel more "privileged", I must admit. It was also rather exciting to explore the seat, after all those times of glancing at it whilst passing by the business class cabin to get to my economy class seat. I felt somewhat uncomfortable when greeted by the flight attendant - "Ms Ng, can I get you a drink?", whilst being offered a hot towel and choice of drink and newspapers. You really felt pampered.

I do not drink (so half the benefits of business class are lost on me) but on that occasion, I accepted a glass of champagne and took a few sips. Then I explored the seat functions, the flight menu, and the inflight entertainment offerings. I must admit, I suddenly felt very grown-up and important. This first experience was rather surreal for someone who grew up in a squalid unit with the sofa and coffee table as my bed for the first 10 years of my life.

I have been on many airlines' lounges and business class flights since then, but nothing beats the excitement of that first flight. Come to think of it, it is somewhat sad that the excitement of visiting the lounge and being in a business class cabin had died down after the initial flights–one get jaded and tired of air travel after years of travelling.

The First Time I Have The Room To Myself

The first time I had a hotel room to myself was when I took a brief trip to Kuala Lumpur. Before then, I always had my Ah Ma as my roommate, so I had never slept alone.

I remembered my parents' advice to do the "knock-knock" on the door before entering the room. It felt strange to be in a room all by myself. After an early dinner, I went to bed but could not sleep. I then started imagining things–what happens if someone breaks into the room? What if the room is haunted?

Eventually I got out of bed and did two things: First, I switched on the bathroom lights and left the bathroom door slightly ajar. Second, I pushed the study chair against the main door, so that if it is opened by an intruder, I should be able to hear some noise and be able to react immediately (of course, I should have realised that this would be an obstacle if I need to evacuate the room in the middle of the night).

With these two moves, I managed to grab some sleep. I kept the practice of keeping the bathroom lights and these 'security lights' as I call them, have enabled me to have a restful sleep for the last two decades of travelling.

Then there was the occasion when I had a hotel suite to myself. There was an entry foyer, a closet, a large bedroom, a work desk, two(!) bathrooms, a living area, a dining area, a bar area, and a powder room. The entire room must have been at least 500 square feet in size, and way too large for my purposes. It got me thinking that if there was someone hiding in the room, it would not be easy to spot the intruder! Before retiring for the night, I had to switch off many sets of lights in different parts of the room and close two sets of doors before I entered the bedroom. I guess I am not meant for the high life, as I certainly did not know how to appreciate it.

The First Time I Planted A Tree

One interesting "first" in my business trips was when I planted a tree in Brazil, São Paulo! This happened on my trip to a company which owned a plantation producing biofuel from sugar cane (it was also the first time I took a private small plane to reach a work destination). It surprised my boss and I when we were led to a patch of land with a line of young trees, each with a name tag on it. We were then each given a small tree sapling and a spade, and we planted our trees! I had never planted a tree before (or since), and having one planted in my name thousands of miles away from Singapore was a cool act. Better still, two years later, my boss sent me a photo of the trees when he was there on a recent trip (I had moved on to a new role). My tree was growing taller than his, and he was jealous. "Woman's touch", I told him.

The First Time I Conducted An Interview In Mandarin

I was in Beijing to conduct an internal assurance exercise (2nd Line of Defence in risk management) for a business line. It was to be conducted in English, over a period of two days, with interviews lined up with about a dozen colleagues.

After the first interview, I realised that whilst the colleague could speak English, he was not comfortable speaking it for the entire duration of the interview, and his replies were rather short and at surface level. I thus could not get an in-depth understanding of his replies and that would not help me with my goal.

I then attempted to conduct the interview in mandarin and enlisted the help of a colleague to translate some common business terms I used in the interview into mandarin. Whilst I am rather articulate in mandarin, my fluency is pegged more for social settings and not so much for a business conversation. Nevertheless, it worked, and the subsequent interviews went well. It pleased most colleagues that the interview was in mandarin, and it also quickly bridged the gap between us, and the interviewee could rattle off his or her views freely. Of course, I could not converse fully in mandarin, and for some terms I had to use a mix of English and mandarin, but it sure worked nicely. I spent the evening revising some of the more difficult Chinese words and the second day of interviews went swimmingly well. It was a fun and enriching experience, and I thoroughly enjoyed this "first"!

The First Time I Attended A Board Dinner

Another "first" was attending a board meeting for the first time (this was the eventful trip in chapter 9 - Of Missing Trains and Flights), and it included a banquet. A formal Chinese dinner is an interesting affair. Guests sit around an enormous round dining table, and lots of dishes are being brought in. I was awed by the amount of food presented – there was no way we would be able to polish them off. The dinner started with the VIPs giving their speeches. After which, I thought dinner would begin, but it was strange, as after a few mouthfuls, the men started getting out of their seats, moving from person to person to toast a drink, using bai-jiu, a high-alcohol spirit, or wine. The men were forgiving towards those like me who do not drink - I took a courtesy sip for each toast offered. "It's ok, one does one's best", my colleague said when I apologized I could not "gan bei" with him. It was amusing to see the drinking going around the room. Hardly anyone touched their food, and I was thus embarrassed to eat my fill, hence returning to the room at the end of the night with a hungry stomach and had to make do with my biscuits. I learned a lesson that night. Eat sufficiently to fill your stomach before going to a banquet.

The First Time I Was On A First-Class Cabin

I had the opportunity to fly in a first-class cabin on two business trips (though I have also travelled on first-class flights during my expatriate days, courtesy of the generous travel allowances). Both were Singapore Airlines (SQ) flights, and I was thrilled as I have travelled first-class with the national airline and was keen to see how flying first class with SQ would be.

Upon reaching the First-Class Check-in Reception at Terminal 3(T3), I was immediately greeted by the Relations Officer, who offered me a seat whilst she printed my ticket. A porter then took my luggage, and I was led to the exclusive immigration processing station nearby. Another few steps and after walking through a door, I was already in the T3 passenger terminal, right in front of the escalator that led to the SQ lounge. The Private Room lounge looked exclusive and was true to its name, with a restaurant set-up and only a handful of passengers. Overall, the lounge was great, but to be honest, I felt it was on par, but not better than some other first-class lounges I visited before.

In the cabin, the seat and the menu were obviously different and better than that offered in the business class cabin, and each passenger was given an amenity bag - containing a scented candle, lip balm, body lotion, and soap. Frankly, if the ticket was on my own account, I would not have felt that the price delta between a first and business class ticket to be worth its premium, but that's just my thoughts.

Well, unfortunately, that trip was dampened by me somehow getting a bed bug bite which showed up when I arrived in my hotel room. I could not fathom where I could have gotten it, as it could have bitten me on the taxi ride to the airport, at the lounge, on the plane, or on the taxi ride to the hotel. Maybe it is telling me I am not meant for first-class. In any case, two SQ first-class flight experiences were enough for me. And I have the amenity kits to remind me of them.

The First Time I Was The Only Female In The Room

To begin with, there is usually a higher proportion of males in the room for most of the meetings I attend. It is even less common to have an Asian in a European or American meeting setting. I was quite oblivious to the Diversity & Inclusiveness lens previously, but in recent years, I have become more conscious of it and often pondered what it may take to make the workplace more gender and race neutral.

The first time where I was the only female in an external meeting was when I attended a board meeting in a middle east country. Prior to the trip, there were some reservations within my work circle whether my presence may cause discomfort to the local gentlemen, as the country was just opening to have more women participate in the workforce and this may be the first time they see a woman in the boardroom. One senior colleague cautioned me and advised me not to go. I considered what he said for a minute and decided that there was nothing to worry about, and also, my boss would travel with me for this first trip and two other colleagues would also be there.

Well, the trip went well, and the fact that I was a female did not make any difference, I felt. I was advised not to hold out my hand to shake hands when introduced, but to wait and see if the other party held out theirs first, and only if he did, I would then return the handshake. Most of the gents held out their hands when I was introduced to them, and for the few who could not(for religious reasons), there was no awkwardness and we continued to have a pleasant conversation.

On my second trip there, I took the role of the Audit Committee chair and sat at the top of the table. For a minute, I even felt somewhat strange that a female was sitting there flanked by gents on her left and right, but that was it. We got down to business right away.

The First Time I Got Tipsy

As a young adult, I was an occasional social drinker. I could drink a little but took little pleasure from it, so I drank little. As years went by, I started to develop heart palpitations whenever I took more than a few sips, so nowadays I do not touch alcohol at all.

This story happened in the years before I get heart palpitations when I consume alcohol. There was a team meeting held in New Orleans, and when you are there, you must visit the jazz bars, which we went to after dinner one evening.

It was a lovely setup, with an intimate atmosphere and with jazz musicians swooning the audience with their husky voices and swinging saxophones. My boss (this was an interesting man who took a photo from each hotel room window he stayed in—a hobby, he said) ordered alcoholic drinks for everyone, but I was the only one who ordered a glass of orange juice. I was quite content with my drink, but he felt I was missing out and kept asking me if I would like to order one, as he felt one must have a good drink to enjoy a jazz bar fully.

After he asked me for the third time, I sensed his sincerity and ordered a margarita. He was right. It indeed felt different and more atmospheric with a drink in hand. I must have drunk more than I should, as when it was time to pack up and go, I stood up and immediately felt my head spinning and crashed right back onto my seat.

This startled everyone, especially my boss, who then quickly got me a glass of water to drink. The team had to wait for a couple of minutes for my head to get back to order before we could leave the bar.

Yes, it was embarrassing for me, but I think my boss was more uncomfortable than me, as it was he who had insisted that I get a drink. I had a good time anyway, and hey, I drank at a jazz bar, a "first" for me!

First Time I Could Not Switch On The TV Set

The one that won the "first" of the "firsts" experiences must have been the occasion I stayed in a Guangzhou hotel, and despite multiple attempts, I could not get the TV set to work. I was able to switch on the TV set but could not click the correct buttons to get to a TV channel. I was not looking for a specific channel–most times I have the TV on so that there is some "noise" in the room–but on this occasion, all I have was a TV screen with Chinese characters and some still images, but no TV channel came up no matter what I clicked. I gave up after a while and felt like an idiot–have you ever met someone who does not know how to operate a TV set?

I felt better the next morning when I realised many in the team also did not manage to get it to work. The Caucasians in the group said they had a good reason, as they did not understand the instructions of the Chinese characters on the TV screen, but the rest of us could only shrug our shoulders. We finally got to know the tricks on what to click to get to the channels. We also understood from our Chinese colleagues that the company which manufactured this TV brand had gone out of business. I wondered why.

How many of your first-time experiences in business travelling do you remember?

SHARING TIP!

Look back and recount the different "firsts" in your business travelling experiences. You will be amazed at the variety of rich experiences you have accumulated!

Chapter 12

Impact of "Covidaggedon" on Business Travelling

"To Travel Or Not To Travel, That Is The Question."

The world has changed much since the first Covid-19 case was identified in China in late 2019. We are still learning about the insidious virus, praying for it to end soon and that the vaccines can work effectively in preventing us from being infected. For most (if not all) of us, our working and personal lives have changed substantially since the start of 2020, and at this point of writing, the world is still living under the shadows of the virus, and the many changes that it has brought into our lives and economies.

I began working from home in February 2020 and only met up with a few team members and colleagues that whole year. Video conferencing became the dominant form of communication. Accordingly, all business travel was cancelled. I would have made six or seven trips by June 2020, if not for the ban on business travel imposed by my company.

Some meetings were cancelled, while the rest continued as virtual meetings. I was curious to know how much time I had saved by not going on business trips and did a calculation of the estimated door-to-door travelling time of those seven trips (two intercontinental trips and five regional trips, including long-distance road travel). The time I would have spent air-bound or on the road came up to almost 160 hours or six and a half days. I suddenly felt so time rich! And this does not include the volume of carbon emissions reduced by not flying or being on the road.

There are disadvantages to business travelling which the employer and employee should be conscious of:

1. **Cost.** Sum up the cost of land and air transportation, hotel accommodation and meals for each trip, then add the estimated cost on the loss of manpower time while being on the road or flying in the air, which could have been spent on productive work instead. Multiply the cost by the number of times and the number of staff who went on a trip and compare that with the expected economic and qualitative return that trip is to reap—is it a positive NPV (Net Present Value), as one ex-boss of mine would ask?

   Frankly, for most team meetings, besides the feel-good factor and no doubt the benefits from strengthened relationships, I do not feel that the team performance would suffer simply because we could not meet as a team, nor would we become much more effective just because we did. With the global economic impact expected from Covid-19, I would hope that corporations will scrutinize the reason for travel more strongly in the future.

2. **Travel health and safety, and risk exposure** for the employee. Employers want their staff to commute to and from work daily in safety. When an employee travels for work, it is the employer's responsibility to ensure their safety—from the moment they leave their homes to go on a trip, right up to the time they return home. Travelling exposes the staff to several risks - in transportation (e.g., accidents on the road, in the air, at the office, etc.), health (e.g., stress, jetlag, bad diet, lack of exercise), safety (e.g.,

falling on a slippery surface, being robbed, threatened, kidnapped even), and radiation (hundreds of times higher with the plane at high altitude). Today, we face the additional risk of Covid-19 exposure. Everyone sees or imagines the glamour in travelling, but do we cast enough attention on the potential risks it may bring?

3. **Time away from home and commitments.** This can be a parent who wants to guide the children on schoolwork after dinner; the parent who wants to be there to cheer at the children's sports day event; the spouse who wants to be home to support his/her spouse who is having some issues at work or is feeling unwell; the son or daughter who wants to be with dad or mum when they visit the doctor; or the gardener who wants to tend to the house plants (many of my plants died due to lack of tender loving care as a result of my trips). I know we are sometimes happy and may even be secretly glad to step away briefly from personal commitments or have a 'break' from family but at the same time, business travel can take away precious and important moments with loved ones that can never be replaced.

For the 2020 meetings that took place virtually, I did not feel that having them online affected the quality of the team or board meetings. One meeting even achieved a 'personal best' and finished ahead of the scheduled time! Perhaps the quality of these meetings did not suffer as:

· Participants already knew each other, and this familiarity helped in the virtual setting;

- All were accustomed to the meeting's objectives and format;
- Mindful that this was a virtual setup, more pre-engagements were done to allow clarification of questions and to ensure the alignment of meeting objectives;
- Participants were reminded to keep comments crisp and clear;
- Most of us were dialling in from the same time zone. It was not difficult to set a slot which suited Asian and European time zones, though we had a lone American participant who had to dial in at 2 am his time;
- With the advancement of digital meeting platforms, the virtual meeting setups held up well most of the time, though occasionally a participant would suddenly lose connectivity for a short time. (It happened to me once after I had spoken at a meeting and was awaiting a response. An air force fighter jet had flown over my block and momentarily knocked out my Wi-Fi. You do not want to know my reaction.)

Does this mean we can reduce the number of business trips in the future and change our work habits to allow for more flexibility to work from home? The jury is still out, but I believe it is possible. I hope that this worldwide experiment on virtual meetings will force us to constructively challenge the need for business travel in future and not be so "trigger-travel happy".

I recall one trip to London where a lady who was behind me in the queue at Heathrow Airport's Immigration Counter told me she would be in London for just a half day meeting and that she would fly back right after that. She had not wanted to make this trip and honestly did not see the need for it but could not convince her boss to let her dial in instead. "Wow, a 4-hour meeting, and almost 30 hours of travel time," I was bewildered. "Tell me about it!" She was resigned to the situation, but I guessed it must have been a very important meeting that best requires physical attendance.

That said, there are advantages to business travelling which we should also acknowledge:

1. This is probably the most important reason—humans thrive from **face-to-face interaction and connectivity**, and this networking is especially crucial when meeting new contacts, strengthening relationships with important stakeholders like suppliers or customers, resolving a sensitive issue, or bonding as a new team by fostering a sense of unity and collaboration. Employees also value regular visits from senior management. Important face-to-face meetings would also be preferred where there is a language barrier, as it helps to reduce the risk of miscommunication as one can pick up physical cues or the 'elephant in the room'. So far, technology cannot provide the same experience.

2. Travelling opens the eyes of the business traveller to the world, and to experience the different economies, cultures, and societies. It also forces us to be independent, and learn to be more street smart, adaptable and **hopefully gain some life skills** along the way. These are not skills that one can get sitting at home or in the office, and such experiences help to develop a more effective worker and leader.

3. One gets to **see places** one may otherwise not get to visit. If not for my business travels, I would not have managed

to visit a particular middle east country, for example. My company trips have certainly made me a world citizen. Not to mention the air miles gained and the opportunity to travel in a Business or First-Class cabin, I should add.

I hope to see a more productive balance between virtual versus face-to-face meetings post "Covidaggedon". Besides business travel, many of us are also missing our personal overseas holidays, myself included. It has been over a year since my last overseas trip, which was a cruise to Malaysia and Thailand. Our planned trips to Japan and the UK were cancelled. I cannot remember the last time I have stayed put in Singapore for so long. It really felt strange, but when I thought more about this, I realized I had spent the first 15 years of my life in Singapore and had not stepped foot outside its shores until my first trip to Kuala Lumpur. I never felt that I had missed out on anything during those 15 years, nor did I feel it strange to be "stuck" in my homeland. Some food for thought.

Advances in air travel and particularly budget air travel have expanded our travel options, but perhaps it has also led us to think vacations should only be spent overseas. The past year has given us a timely opportunity to get reacquainted with every nook and cranny in Singapore. I have taken many walks in my development's grounds and have discovered the variety of flora we have here, which I had not appreciated before. We have gone on many runs. Our house looks much neater and cleaner. Many of us have also learned to cook new dishes and bake cakes and have started new hobbies like gardening and painting. Any small group gathering now feels like a blessing, and our conversations are more personal. It is amazing how the society can adjust so quickly to new challenges and make the best out of a situation.

Ask and challenge the organiser, "Is this meeting necessary, and if so, can it be done virtually or is face-to-face necessary?"

Chapter 13

Post Business
Travelling Days

*"Do Not Mourn The Day You Lose Your SQ PPS/Solitaire
Status."*

My family and I took our first flight on an overseas trip when I was 15. The air journey took less than an hour, as we were only travelling to Kuala Lumpur (with Genting Highlands as our final destination), but as it was the first time that we were on a plane, everyone was over the moon and excited with the many 'firsts' to be experienced on an overseas trip. We enjoyed every minute of the flight and had a fun and memorable experience in Genting Highlands.

One memory from that trip was meeting an elderly gentleman whilst we were waiting at the departure gate. My parents struck up a conversation with him and then presented the brood to him. When I was introduced to him, he remarked, "Hey, I would have sworn that I saw you in the United States a few weeks ago!"

Now, obviously, he was mistaken, but my parents, especially my mother, were somehow happy that he thought he saw me in a first world country and was beaming at this point. I supposed they felt that being able to travel to a developed and faraway country like the United States was no mean feat, i.e. an impossible dream for the likes of us. She then remarked that hopefully someday I would be there, and the family had a good laugh over this encounter.

My mum must have got some good foresight, for her daughter did subsequently make many business trips to the States. Her son also worked in New York for two years, and she also got to spend a month there, together with my father.

Does travelling abroad move one up the "accomplishment" ladder and make one an "important/VIP" person? Whenever I travel, I would take a quick glance at my fellow passengers in the business class cabin–effects of the boredom factor, as I call it. Usually, the proportion of men to women in the business class cabin is about three to one. Sometimes I would see a young family travelling and I would think, "such lucky kids, travelling in business class at this age!" Occasionally you would see a first-time business class traveller–hard to miss the excitement in their eyes as they fiddled with the remote control and the seat configuration, as I had, many years ago! Then there are the veteran travellers who have got airplane travel down to the T, with their "standard operating procedure" such as changing to lounge clothes once they got on the plane, ordering their standard drink and falling asleep within 15 minutes of take-off.

Most travellers are pleasant and courteous to the crew and to fellow passengers, but I have come across a few who felt that they are a privileged group and have sky-high expectations and demands. I recalled a night flight where there was this chap who gave a stern talking to an SQ stewardess for over 15 minutes shortly after take-off. I did not catch much of the conversation, other than his comment that "I'm a PPS (Priority Passenger Service) member and I do not expect this type of service", which he repeated a few times and hence caught my ear. "What is the big deal about PPS status," I muttered under my breath. I suspect a significant portion of us in that cabin has it, too.

Maybe he had a valid complaint to make, but I felt that he could have done it in an amiable and respectable manner, rather than riding on his airline's membership status and expecting to be treated like a king. What happens then when he loses that status? Surely one cannot expect to hold on to this membership status for life.

The strange world of 2020 (and 2021) has resulted in zero overseas travel for millions and business travel has come to almost a complete stop. Some have bemoaned the loss of their corporate travelling life and the perks it offered, whilst most I suspect are secretly happy that they can now be with their family daily and sleep on their beds and not in a strange hotel room.

My business travelling days came to a stop when I left the company at the end of 2020. I would admit that I had thought about whether I would miss business travelling, especially being able to access the lounge, having comfortable seats and good dining on the plane, and staying in 5 stars hotels. I would be lying if I said I would not miss it at all, but frankly, I do not think it would make a huge dent in my quality and purpose of life!

I have heard of senior executives who suffered withdrawal symptoms and a sense of loss when they no longer travel frequently and hence lost their airline's premium membership status and privileges. Perhaps what they bemoan is the feeling of being important and respected as someone who is "up there" on the career ladder. Being robbed of their work responsibilities and frequent flyer status may cause some to lose their sense of self-worth, which is a shame given the illustrious career they have had.

Thank goodness I have never been one who hankers for such status. Corporate travel does not 'increase' your social standing and flying first class does not mean you are a high-class person.

Well, and all said, I guess I can still fork out my money and buy a business class ticket when I go on vacation if I want a more comfortable journey.

What I will miss, though, is meeting people from different parts of the world and getting to know them better on a personal level. I have been invited to meals in colleagues' homes, met their families, went on walks together, sang and danced on tabletops together, and shared stories about our personal lives. It is interesting to note that we may come from different countries and cultures, but we may be more similar than we think. For example, a few female South African colleagues once shared over dinner they were the first generation in their families to make it to university. Their parents(and extended family) were immensely proud of their achievements, but with that, there is also the implicit expectation that they contribute to the family by giving a portion of their monthly salary and helping to take care of the younger generation.

I shared that this is similar to the Asia practice of giving monthly allowance to our parents and helping the extended family where possible. We all agreed that we gave willingly, and that it was the right thing to do—family first! Stories like these make business travelling fascinating and enriching, and such human-to-human social interactions bring colour and richness to one's life experiences.

Cheers to business travelling post Covid-19!

Be conscious that you will not get to hold onto your favourite airline's frequent flyer membership status for life. Be prepared for life post "PPS/ Solitaire status".

Chapter 14

Epilogue

Whether it was a long or a brief business trip, one thing I used to enjoy on the return flight was to look out of the window as the plane flew into Singapore territory and prepared for its touchdown.

If it was a day flight, I soaked in the sights of the Singapore skyline, with its busy roads and skyscrapers, and ships of different sizes parked in the harbour. If it was a night flight, the sky would be aglow with streetlights, the lights streaming from vehicles and from the homes of 1.37 million households[21], presenting a stunning and breath-taking view of our beautiful city. As we approached Changi Airport, a warm and secure feeling would build up, as I knew I was almost on home ground.

The best moment had always been when the SQ plane touched down on the runway at Changi Airport, and the flight attendant would make the famous passenger announcement. "Welcome to Singapore, Ladies and Gentlemen. And to all Singaporeans and residents of Singapore, a warm welcome home." I have heard this line many times, but each time, it has never failed to warm the cockles of my heart, and I get the snuggly feeling of home and of loved ones looking to welcome me back.

The world is our oyster, and there is a lot to see, learn and to gain by leaving our shores and exploring different countries and every nook and cranny from different corners of this world.

But at the end of the day, Singapore is where we call home, and homeward bound we will always be, no matter how far we have ventured out.

"This is home truly,
where I know I must be
Where my dreams wait for me,
where the river always flows
This is home surely, as my senses tell me
This is where I won't be alone,
for this is where I know it's home."
~ Home, composed by Dick Lee, performed by Kit Chan

Chapter 15

Appendix: Tips for a Safe and Smooth Business Travel

"When Preparing To Travel, Lay Out All Of Your Clothes And All Of Your Money. Then Take Half The Clothes And Twice The Money. – Susan Heller"

1. **Store your Emergency Contact List in your wallet/passport or somewhere easy for others to find**

   Once on a flight from the UK to Singapore, an announcement was made that a passenger needed medical attention and requested any doctors or medical personnel on board to come forward. One always gets a knot in the stomach when you hear such announcements made. I said a quiet prayer for the passenger. We heard later that he was a young man travelling alone. It then dawned on me it would be useful to have the contact details of my next of kin in a place that would be easy for the crew to find so that my family could be contacted immediately if needed.

2. **Take some "energy" snacks with you**

   You never know when you may need them! In the above-mentioned flight, it was suspected that the passenger had suffered a heart attack. As the situation was serious, the plane diverted from its scheduled route and made its way to the nearest airport. We saw the whole works—ambulances, fire engines, and then the de-icing of the plane as it was snowing outside (I waved at the firefighter who waved back). It took three hours or so before we could get back on the air, by which time the cabin crew apologized, saying they could not serve the hot meals for food safety reasons. We got through the rest of the journey with just potato chips, nuts, and fruits.

It is also helpful to have some of your favourite snacks with you as comfort food for long journeys, and in case you miss home!

3. **Copy of your passport**

   Useful to make a few copies of your passport page just in case you lose your passport. It is also recommended to email a copy to yourself and to save it in a secure folder so that you have easy access to a soft copy.

4. **Share your travel plans**

   Give a copy of your travel details (flight /hotel /itinerary /travel insurance policy /overseas contact) to a family member so that at any one point, someone knows your travel plans and details.

5. **Credit Card details**

   Ensure you have a copy of your credit card details, including the contact number of the financial institution. Always have at least two cards with you in case one does not work for any reason.

6. **Travel insurance**

   My company provides us with travel insurance whenever we travel on business. When I go on private trips, or if I extend my business trip for personal reasons, I will purchase a travel insurance plan. In fact, if I expect a particular year to be a year of heavy travel, I will buy an annual travel insurance plan, to save myself the effort of going online to buy insurance before each trip.

   Having insurance gives you the comfort that should anything untoward happen, you will get financial support and assistance needed. Always have the number for emergency medical support and travel assistance on hand.

7. **Carry extra cash**

   Most things are cashless nowadays, but cash is still king, and it is handy to have some extra cash on hand for unforeseen events. See my story on the impact of Hurricane Rita—I would have been in trouble if I had not managed to leave Houston in time, as I had taken very little cash with me on that trip. With US dollars being an international currency, it is always helpful to have some US dollar notes on hand.

8. **Use carry-on cabin luggage**

   Whenever possible, use carry-on luggage. This allows you to zip out of the airport immediately, and your luggage will never be lost! It saves a lot of time.

9. **What to pack**

   I pack light for business trips, with versatile clothing (I have designated some of my work clothes as 'travel' wear). I have a toiletries pouch set aside for travel. Other stuff used solely for business trips are washed/wiped after a trip and go straight back into the cabin luggage. This saves a lot of time when packing for a trip—I am sure no one enjoys this part of the trip preparation!

10. **Water bottle**

    Be it a personal or business trip, I always carry a water bottle or vacuum flask with me, which I will fill up at the airport's water cooler before getting on the plane. Important to stay hydrated in the air, and upon hopping off the plane, it may take hours before you reach your destination, so having some water to sip is essential!

11. **First aid kit**
    Always carry some basic medicine with you—paracetamol, band-aids, pills for indigestion, diarrhoea, motion sickness, and cold tablets. You never know when you or someone around you may need them.

12. **Cardigan/Sweater/Scarf**
    The airplane can get incredibly cold. I always have at least a scarf and a sweater with me on board the plane. They have proved to be handy on several occasions!

13. **Plan for a time buffer to get to the airport**
    There are at least two groups of people when it comes to time buffers. The first group applies a "just in time('JIT')" approach and will appear at the gate just before it closes. The second group applies a "no rush" approach and will be at the airport with ample time to spare. Just ensure both groups do not travel together. A colleague who was clearly from the second group recounted her experience travelling with someone from the first group. "I've never been so stressed in my life," she recounted, "and it was mightily embarrassing to hear our names being announced over the loudspeaker telling us to get onto the plane now!"
    Another "JIT" colleague shared that he normally arrives at Changi Airport with just enough time to go to the gate before it closes. However, one eventful day, there was a major traffic accident on the road, and that part of the highway was fully jammed. He ended up missing the flight.
    I belong to the second group. I prefer a stressless journey to the airport and like to relax in the lounge or browse through the shops. Bottom line is, 'JIT' may not work all the time, so having some time buffer is helpful.
    That said, unplanned events do happen, and learning to

keep calm and staying zen and sane is important. I am still learning to accomplish this.

14. **Seatbelts on**

Do you always keep your seatbelt fastened throughout the flight (even when the seatbelt sign has been turned off)? I do. Always. We have read enough stories of what can happen during air turbulence. I have even told strangers to do so (e.g. I encouraged Kate, from Chapter 6 to refasten her belt when she unfastened hers after the seat-belt sign went off), as I am concerned for their safety.

My company's policy also mandates that we must have our seatbelt on when travelling in vehicles, and that we are not to travel in any vehicle, be it a bus or car, that does not have seat belts installed. To me, this is a basic safety practice which we can do to protect ourselves and be a responsible traveller. Some may see this as an inconvenience, but always remember, your life is worth more than the so-called inconvenience.

15. **Airplane safety instructions**

Most safety videos may not be entertaining to watch, but it is important that you pay attention to them, know where your nearest exit point is, and count the number of seats to that exit. I also make sure I know where the safety vest is.

Some smaller planes have the flight attendant to demonstrate the safety instructions. I would usually cast my eyes upon them to show rapport and give them some support, as most passengers seem to ignore such demonstrations, and I would not want them to think that no one is watching when they are demonstrating such an important briefing.

16. Arrival plans

You may arrive at your destination at an unearthly hour, and hence it is important to make arrival plans. For most of my business trips, a pickup is usually arranged, and all I need to do is to pray that the driver will show up on time and that I will be able to find him or her. There have been a few times when I was at the wrong meeting point, or the driver was late.

One safety check I do is to ask the driver where he is taking me—to make sure I am getting into the right car. Keep your wits about you all the time, especially if you are travelling alone.

17. When travelling in a car

It can be tempting to have a snooze when you get into a car and the destination is a good 30 minutes or so away. Even more so when you have just hopped off from a long flight.

Tempting as it is, do not fall asleep! Be aware of your surroundings. It also helps the driver to have someone to chat with, especially if you are travelling in the early or late hours of the day. Your driver may get tired and fall asleep at the wheel. I have experienced this once or twice, and I shudder to think what may have happened if I had been asleep!

18. Fire exits

Upon checking into your hotel room, what do you do first? As per company guidelines, I check out where the fire exit route is from my room and count the number of doors from my room to the fire exit.

If a fire breaks out the next minute or in the middle of the night, it helps if you already have a mind map and know whether to head left or right to evacuate. It pays to be pre-pared!

19. **Hand sanitiser**

Maybe I have a bit of obsessive-compulsive disorder, but even pre Covid-19, I always carried a bottle of hand sani-tiser when I travelled. I used it (or the hot towel given) to wipe the seats, TV screen, remote control, and serving tray on the plane.

When I step into my hotel room, after checking the fire exits, the next thing I do is to apply hand sanitiser and wipe the toilet bowl, the room phone, and the TV remote control. Only then do I unpack my stuff. This is my stan-dard operating procedure indeed!

20. **Travel Preparation Checklist**I have a small checklist which I do a quick check against before leaving for the air-port. It caters to the different seasons. Here it is:

Items	In Luggage?
Wallet, passport, ticket	
Camera	
Pen and notebook	
Extra bag(foldable)	
Phone charger/laptop charger/ headset/adaptor	
Snacks and water bottle	
Work shoes/socks/slippers	
Wet tissues/tissue paper	
Umbrella/cap	
Toiletries	
Swimsuit/suntan lotion/ mosquito repellent	
Sweater, scarf, lightweight jacket	
Clothes/underwear/Pyjamas	
Book	
Coffee/tea sachets	

Extra pair of spectacles/
sunglasses
Medicine bag

Earmuff, heat pad

Shopping bag (be environment
friendly, BYO)

Lock and key

Bedroom slippers
(be environment friendly, BYO)

Reusable utensils (be
environment friendly, BYO)

Face mask *(a must post-Covid-19,
but was also useful pre-Covid-19*

ENDNOTES:

1. "How Much Airline Revenue Comes From Business Travelers?", Investopedia Team, Updated 28 May 2021

2. "42 Business Travel Statistics That Will Inspire You to Hit the Road", Danica Jovic, smallbizgenius.net, Updated 11 Jan 2021

3. "Why Does Chocolate Make Us Happy?", Sather Health, 20 Feb 2014

4. "Does chocolate make you happy?", Science Focus

5. "Science Reveals Surprising Connection Between Chocolate and Love", Gabe Bergado, 4 Dec 2014

6. "Is Ginger a Safe and Effective Treatment for Nausea?", Lauren Panoff, MPH, RD, 29 Aug 2019

7. "Naomi Campbell's in-flight sanitizing routine seemed extreme — until now", Chrissy Callahan, 6 Mar 2020

8. "Why Do I Get Motion Sickness?", WedMD, Medically Reviewed by Dan Brennan, MD on 11 Aug 21, 2020

9. "Balut, the terrifying hard-boiled duck fetus that's also a tasty aphrodisiac", M. Paramita Lin, 31 Oct 2016

10. "Jet Lag", Medicinenet, John P. Cunha, DO, FACOEP, *18 Nov 2019*

11. "The military secret to falling asleep in two minutes", Independent Staff, 1 Sep 2021
12. "How the 5 Pillars of Life Help You Achieve Balance and Fulfillment", Defyandhustle.com
13. "The 5 Pillars of a Happy, Abundant Life", Luke Rowley, 26 Jan 26, 2019
14. "If You Always Do What You've Always Done, You Always Get What You've Always Gotten", Jessie Potter
15. "Regrets of the Dying", Bronnie Ware
16. "Hurricane Katrina: Facts, Damage & Aftermath", Kim Ann Zimmermann, 28 Aug 2015
17. "Evacuees burn to death on bus in exodus gridlock", Julian Borger and Jamie Wilson, 24 Sep 2005
18. "Bleisure travel", Wikipedia
19. "What is Bleisure Travel? What Are Bleisure Travellers Looking For?", Revfine.com
20. "How Andersen binds its people", Tim Boreham, 6 Aug 1993
21. "Number of households in Singapore from 2011 to 2020 (in millions)", Statista.com